T0194233

ENDORSEMENTS

"Alex Mirza's research provides compelling insights for what hospitality stakeholders must do to build human capital and achieve a higher purpose in these extraordinary times. It is not just recommended reading, it is required."

—Geoff Ballotti, President & CEO, Wyndham Hotels & Resorts, and recipient of the Arne Sorenson Social Impact Leadership Award.

"Alex Mirza has taken that step and advanced our understanding of how to use the new technology tools to address the considerable operational issues facing service firms. This is an absolute must read!"

—Leonard A. Schlesinger, Baker Foundation Professor, Harvard Business School and co-author of landmark bestseller *The Service Profit Chain*

"A fascinating new study into the challenges facing the industry in an era increasingly being labeled by some scholars as one of "de-globalization.""

—David G. Haglund, Professor of Political Studies, Queen's University (Canada)

"Our industry faces a foundational challenge in rethinking traditional business models to rebuild our talent pipeline and, once again, become an employer of choice. As one of hospitality's most innovative thought leaders, Alex's work comes at a pivotal time, providing much-needed, research-based answers to the most critical questions facing today's travel and tourism executives."

—Adam Burke, CEO, LA Tourism Council & Convention Board

"With its cutting-edge insights on AI-driven solutions and employee empowerment, this book paves the way for a revolutionary approach to using artificial intelligence to innovate business models in travel and hospitality. Discover your blueprint for success in this indispensable read."

—Anita Gupta, Forbes 50 Over 50 Entrepreneur; Founder, KiwiTech

REIMAGINING GLOBAL HOSPITALITY

ENVISAGING THE AI HOTEL OF THE FUTURE

Alexander Mirza

ARCHWAY
PUBLISHING

Archway Publishing books may be ordered through booksellers or by contacting:

Archway Publishing
1663 Liberty Drive
Bloomington, IN 47403
www.archwaypublishing.com
844-669-3957

Because of the dynamic nature of the Internet, any web addresses or links contained in this book may have changed since publication and may no longer be valid. The views expressed in this work are solely those of the author and do not necessarily reflect the views of the publisher, and the publisher hereby disclaims any responsibility for them.

Cover Designer: Irene Birgita Derru

ISBN: 978-1-6657-5480-4 (sc)
ISBN: 978-1-6657-5482-8 (hc)
ISBN: 978-1-6657-5481-1 (e)

Library of Congress Control Number: 2024900527

Print information available on the last page.

Archway Publishing rev. date: 01/16/2024

BOOK DESCRIPTION

This book provides a strategic roadmap creating the next generation of global hospitality brands and experiences that create economic wealth and make a difference in the world. It provides insights into using new technologies such as artificial intelligence and virtual reality to innovate the customer experience, restore meritocracy in the workplace and diversify economies with sustainable indigenous tourism. The author shares a blueprint for the AI hotel of the future and progressive systems of corporate, national and international AI governance in a turbulent, multi-polar world.

KEYWORDS AND PHRASES

Artificial Intelligence; Brand Management; Innovation; Sustainable Development; Hospitality Management; National Competitiveness;

CONTENTS

Foreword xi

Acknowledgements xiii

Preface: Summoning A New Generation of Leadership xv

1   Building Brands with a Purpose. 1

2   Beyond the Golden Age of Travel. 13

3   Beating the Talent Disruption. 37

4   Envisaging the AI Hotel of the Future
    (Co-authors: Sahar Cain, Gurvinder Batra) 48

5   Overturning Orthodoxies to Accelerate Diversity 65

6   Replenishing America's Talent Engine 74

7   Canada as a Tourism Superpower 93

8   Mougulan Seeking Extraordinary Talent in China 114

Epilogue: A Call to Action: Responsible AI. 141

Co-Authors. 151

Resources and References 153

FOREWORD

At KiwiTech, we believe in the power of technology to create new wealth and social change. Over the past 15 years, our experience building a global portfolio of over 600 startups across various sectors, including many led by women, minorities, and economically disadvantaged people, has reinforced what self-made American entrepreneur John D. Rockefeller said to aspiring disruptors: "if you want to succeed you should strike out on new paths, rather than travel the worn paths of accepted success."

Whether it's "revenge travel" or what economists call "pent up demand," the post-pandemic resurgence of travel proves that it's anything but a discretionary luxury: travel is the therapeutic glue that binds people together. It is with great enthusiasm that I write this foreword to "Reimagining Global Hospitality: Building the AI Hotel of the Future," authored by Alexander Mirza, a leader of one of our portfolio companies and our strategic advisor in the fast-changing travel and hospitality space. As the CEO of a global technology and professionals services firm anchored by over 400 diverse technologists in India working to advance responsible artificial intelligence, KiwiTech, is deeply immersed in the various subject matters shared in this book.

Distinguished entrepreneurs can envisage the future. Over the last 15 years, we've witnessed the most successful ones are usually not the media-hyped kids who dropped out of college to start a new venture in their parents' garage. It's the ones who have toiled long hours learning from industry leaders in the establishment, identifying "white spaces" that exist and "connecting the dots" between unarticulated customer needs, new business models and burgeoning but unproven technologies. With his decades of international experience working in senior management roles in travel and hospitality, Alexander Mirza has the perspicacity to correctly diagnose the problems afflicting the travel and hospitality industry. Moreover, in this compelling narrative, Alexander's prognostication of the future has crystal clear implications not just for technology leaders but for all stakeholders, including governments and civil society. He offers solutions for building a sustainable hospitality industry, both from an environmental and human capital perspective and leveraging AI to empower the workforce. Alexander also provides new perspectives on solving some of the most acute problems facing both legacy companies who employ over 300 million people and for the progressive architects of a new generation of sustainable brands and disruptive technologies.

This book goes beyond the typical discourse on technology's role in the future of business. As you engage with "Reimagining Global Hospitality," you are invited to explore the many possibilities that artificial intelligence brings to the forefront of a revitalized travel and hospitality industry. The insights provided in this book, including the practical perspectives provided by Mogul's Chief Technology Officer, Sahar Cain, and our Chief Technology Officer, Gurvinder Batra, provide a roadmap for a future where new technologies advance environmental stewardship, human capital, diversity, equity and inclusion to overcome geopolitical challenges in a more disputatious world.

Welcome to the future of travel and hospitality.

Rakesh Gupta
CEO, KiwiTech

ACKNOWLEDGEMENTS

I cannot express enough gratitude to current and former colleagues for their hard work and dedication to this project. This diverse and talented team collaborated on a number of fronts, from data science and writing algorithms to testing hypotheses and making predictions that made it possible to generate insights using big data gathered from numerous sources. I am also grateful for the contributions of our Chief Technology Officer Sahar Cain, our Economist Nadiia Kudriashova, Ph.D. (Odessa, Ukraine); My former partner at Cachet hotels and our finance advisor Martin Key (Miami, FL); Kiwitech's CEO Rakesh Gupta (New York, NY), CTO Gurvinder Batra (New Delhi, India) and Co-Founder Anita Gupta (Washington DC); my long-time Chinese legal advisor and scholar, Xiang Wei (Beijing, China); fellow Canadian HBS grad Noel Desautels (Toronto, Canada); and the contributions of many family members, most notably my wife, Barbara Mirza (Partner, Cooley LLC Los Angeles).

Finally, to the many software clients around the globe who gave practical feedback on the algorithms and analytics that underpin hospitality's first AI-powered talent marketplace including hotel CEOs, CHROs, CIOs, hotel owners and advisory board members of Mogul Hotels, my heartfelt thanks.

PREFACE
SUMMONING A NEW GENERATION
OF LEADERSHIP

I have been blessed in my 30-year career to have worked in an elite strategy consulting firm owned by one of the leading thought leaders of our generation where we advised CEOs, heads of state and rising stars on breakthrough innovations that would shape their industries and countries for decades to come. I have also served as head of strategic planning and corporate development to four Fortune 500 companies, including reporting directly to three CEOs, one of which is a Harvard Business School professor prior to becoming the CEO of a China based luxury hospitality company and a venture backed company advancing artificial intelligence in travel.

Some of these companies I worked at such as Starwood Hotels and Ticketmaster Entertainment were "deal driven" from the top with core competencies in lifestyle branding, mergers and acquisitions, and capital markets. Others like Hilton Worldwide and Caesars Entertainment were more process-focused, excelling at building organic growth pipelines and more consensus based decision models, capital committees and consultation.

Over the years I learned that culture and strategy are symbiotic. It's essential for CEOs to set a strategic direction but few businesses lend themselves to traditional strategic planning. The process of developing and executing a strategy is itself a process of innovation and hence iterative. Differences in culture between firms should not be confused with whether management had a strategy in place or the merits of a top-down or more organic approach to creating economic value and mobilizing a diverse array of stakeholders including employees, governments, and distribution partners. To the contrary, the competing strategies developed and implemented by the CEOs of these and other travel and hospitality firms generally fell into one of three buckets: (1) real-estate driven, betting on a concentration of typically large, opportunistically branded full service assets in high barrier to entry markets and riding the wave of cyclicality to generate large cash flows that offset capital intensity; (2) distribution technology focused, investing in reservations, loyalty programs and customer relationship management to generate high marginal returns on growth through franchising brands rather than owning or operating them; and (3) people-focused, with outsized investments in customer service, human capital, front-line employee ownership and the service profit chain as a whole. Starwood was an example of the first strategy; Hilton - the second; and Caesars - the third. Competitive rivalry was intense; worldviews differed and the evidence suggested the equity markets were trying to figure out who the real winner would be in the long run as economic globalization opened markets like China, the Middle East to a wave of unprecedented travel and hospitality development that required the participation of Western brands.

Some readers may ask why travel and hospitality companies face such strategic trade-offs. After all, many of America's best companies today – such as Apple, Tesla, Walmart, and Amazon – own retail stores, service centers, warehouses and more while investing heavily in consumer-facing marketplace technology platforms. For example, it can be argued that the people centric strategy in travel and hospitality required significant cutting-edge investments in technology infrastructure and digital marketing. While it's possible, the data doesn't validate such arguments. To oversimplify, the answer can be found in the relatively inferior quality of management in travel and hospitality, the short-term orientation of the investor base which includes a certain type of private equity and the distortions created by family office shareholding structures. In short, management either didn't have the requisite skills and capabilities to build something more integrated and comprehensive and, or, their short-term focused shareholders lacked the risk appetite and patience.

Today, the brick and mortar travel and hospitality sector, which employs 300 million people globally (1 out of 10) and accounts for 10% of global GDP, is a laggard in innovation, wealth creation and social impact. Boards and C-suite executives perpetuate orthodoxies (widely held conventional beliefs about how to manage the business), taking their cue from an insular community of financiers, attorneys, consultants, technology vendors, architects, designers, media and public relations executives. Corporate strategies have converged to the point of being indistinguishable.

The consequences are clearly visible in the numbers. Google, Booking.com, and Airbnb have captured the lion's share of economic value in the capital markets. 5 out of 6 employees in the U.S. work for third party operators (third party contractor firms); hotel assets are sold once every 5.5 years; homogenous brands are commoditizing; customer service is at record lows; labor unions are imposing work rules that depress talent while gaining traction into franchised operations; sustainability gains have been modest and embodied carbon in construction of hotels is a major cause of greenhouse gasses; diversity, equity, and inclusion targets face major gaps at the hotel General Manager level where only 1.5% are Black people; Governments such as those in Canada are taxing the hotel sector by over a $1 billion more than its profits and wasting millions on marketing that's become the subject of meme jokes on social media; digital walls are rising impacting global brand marketing; and travel globalization is on the retreat as witnessed by the exit from Russia and the decline in Chinese outbound travel; business travel has permanently shrunk in part due to companies such as Microsoft and Apple measuring the carbon impact of its employees.

Furthermore, as globalization heads towards disputatiousness and the primacy of America's "benign hegemony" comes to an end, the organizing principles and shared practices that supported the growth of travel and hospitality are being fundamentally challenged.

At its core, travel is supposed to advance learning and cultural understanding between people from different civilizations. However, the travel industry only recently started to market educational and eco-tourism and its principal proponents are vacation rental platforms such as Airbnb and niche expedition providers as opposed to global airlines and hotel chains. Skeptics contend, globalization's failure is metastasizing to travel and hospitality, which reflects a misguided belief that global brands, economic interdependence and cultural exchanges between people and civilizations will lead to peace and security.

These challenges call for a new generation of industry leadership that can capitalize on the convergence of industries accelerated by artificial intelligence and the urgent need for travel and hospitality firms to contribute to sustainability, indigenous travel and eco-tourism, human rights and international peace and security. Artificial intelligence and robotics, innovations in genomics, biotech and personalized medicine that may increase human life expectancy to 120 and new climate technologies are achieving breakthroughs that will become scalable in the years to come.

Employees are still the most critical component of the AI hotel of the future. Without the expertise and creativity of the hotel staff who are part-owners of the property and compensated for their creation of intellectual property, building the AI hotel of the future will be impossible. Humanoid robot branding, which has captured the world's attention, is the next frontier in lifestyle hospitality. This is why the Talent Engine is the core of this operating model, where talents can demonstrate their creativity, and skills and can use resources and experiential learning tools to constantly learn and contribute back to the AI ecosystem by training and enhancing the language models and delivering service innovations. As hotel managers evolve from static programming of their properties to content creators in a world of AI-powered entertainment, new revenue models are created including streaming events and partnering with studios to create pulse-racing, spine-tingling material to communities that relish drama. In the process, the stars of the show such as celebrity chefs, event planners and their teams can receive a share of the royalties.

As quantum computing progresses, industries are converging. Like most disruptive technologies, AI hotels will benefit from learning and collaboration with industries at the cutting edge of robotics and automation such as the hospitals of the future which are pioneering. For example, healthcare is shifting from hospital-based care to lower acuity sites and home-based care, enabled by innovative technologies. In the future, thousands of talents can train Large Language Models and develop humanoids with different service styles and personalities.

As a case in point, advanced computer vision, including the processing abilities of its visual and voice sensors - the robots' nerves and sensory organs - are rapidly advancing with machine learning across sectors including healthcare, education and delivery and logistics such as Amazon's warehouse robots. More power-dense batteries have made it possible for a humanoid robot to move its legs quickly enough to balance dynamically and navigate stairs, ramps and unsteady ground.

I wrote this book because it is my idealistic hope that those out of vogue "global citizens," as the Chief Disruption Officer Donald Trump (ironically a former hotelier himself) calls them, will rise to the occasion and reimagine the travel and hospitality industry and propel all of us to new heights. As artificial intelligence continues to progress at a breathtaking pace, the line between science fiction and reality becomes increasingly blurred. The dawn of AI-driven hospitality is going to reshape travel in ways we could not imagine a few years ago.

When I was growing up, my parents told me, 'Finish your dinner. People in China and India are starving.' I tell my daughters, 'Finish your homework. People in India and China are starving for your job.'

Thomas Friedman

1

BUILDING BRANDS
WITH A PURPOSE

Globalization as we know it, may be coming to an end. The U.S. led world order and economic freedom are rapidly eroding, with huge implications for global hospitality and travel brands. Wars in the Middle East and Ukraine are flashpoints in an unstable, multipolar world where control over companies that command technological superiority and elite talent has become the focal point. In the second half of 2023, Beijing banned iPhones for government officials despite their production in China and Apple's creation of 5 million jobs in the country. China's retaliation is symptomatic of a disintegration of a stable world order in a new Hobbesian technology war of "all against all." New sweeping regulations such as U.S. restrictions on public and private technology investments in China in the areas of advanced computing chips and microelectronics, quantum technology and artificial intelligence prohibit cross-border flows and specifically target "intangible benefits" such as managerial expertise and talent networks. U.S.-based venture capital investment in Chinese tech start-ups have plummeted to $1.2 billion in the first 10 months of 2023 from $9.7 billion in 2022 and $32.9 billion in 2021. Rising digital walls and semiconductor sanctions are fueling an AI arms race where countries such as Germany and Russia are seeking "technology sovereignty," amidst rising anti-immigration sentiments even towards highly skilled talent despite historic labor shortages. The pandemic accelerated a discontinuity, taking us from universalism to tribalism, as democracy and immigration continue to backslide in the face of religio-politics, populism, and irredentism. What's underneath the annihilation of socially popular technology companies such as Apple and TikTok is a "clash of civilizations," where an expanded NATO and its Indo-Pacific allies are confronting a rising Sino-Russian-GCC partnership committed to fighting an artificial intelligence driven arms race.

● Challenges in a Multi-Polar World

Some observers have suggested that post-U.S. hegemony the world is faced with two foreseeable problems, the first of which is nationalism and ethnic strife. Specifically, the aggressive intensification of pent-up nationalisms and the proliferation of inter-ethnic and inter-communal conflicts has called into question George HW Bush's so-called "new world order," which was based on "consultation and cooperation in international organizations." In this setting, Brexit, the relative economic decline of the United States, and the growing illegitimacy of rising challenger states (such as China and India) has worsened the international community's capacity to deal collectively with already aggravated regional conflicts. For instance, the emergence of war-torn new entities out of states such as the former Soviet Union offers a telling illustration of what historian Augustus Norton calls "irredentist campaigns," and political scientist James Rosenau terms "sub-groupism." In response to these developments, the UN Security council of the late 21st century is being forced to cope with the tragic resurgence of ethnic, religious, and tribal conflicts across the globe.

The external management of these rising nationalisms is often made more difficult by the presence of militant, religious radicalism. As military expenditures continue to generate a disproportionately large allotment of income in the developing world, Egyptian political scientist Saad E. Ibrahim most succinctly outlines the new security problem after U.S. hegemony: "each society is going back to the delayed items of the agenda: how to divide or distribute power, to distribute wealth, to distribute prestige." Civil conflicts based on ethnic and religious affiliations, such as those between the Palestinians and Israelis, Rohingya in Myanmar and Uighurs in China, and Azerbaijanis and Armenians in the post- Soviet republics, are often cases where political compromise and third-party mediation becomes especially difficult. As well, the pre- eminence of Islamic fundamentalism as a political religion has provided yet another nationalist "mobilization platform," for anti- Western movements. All of this is to say that the resurgence of religio-politics, the explosion of ethnic enmities and new attitudes towards authority suggest that instability has become the central problem of the 2020s.

A second group of factors shaping the 2020s security dilemma are associated with the frailty of new democracies and the emergence of collapsing states. Already, Libya, Sudan and Venezuela are amongst those heading the extending list of states, where "Lebanonization," or extreme internal fragmentation in the forms of civil strife, government collapse and overwhelming economic deprivation has demanded a peace-imposing response from the international community. Additionally, problems of governability also characterize fledgling democracies in Latin America, Asia, the Middle East, and Africa. Overall, it seems evident that the effectiveness of governments has become increasingly based on the ability of national political agents to meet the cultural and material needs of their sometimes-troubled peoples.

Similarly, others have portrayed the nationalist virus in their outline of "the failed nation state," characterized by civil strife, government breakdown, economic privation, refugee flows, and massive abuses of human rights matched by the evidence that their problems tend to spread to neighboring states. Indeed, there is mounting evidence to support the contention that across the globe well-armed insurgents are causing civil strife, often compounded by natural disasters, inexperienced governments, and limited economic prospects. Scholars from various disciplines have already documented the consequences of these developments, often culminating in a wholesale disruption of essential central government services, food supplies and distribution networks, and the bringing of economies to a virtual standstill.

In this setting, the doomsday predictions offered by both economists and environmentalists are very troubling. They argue that over the next thirty years, the earth's population will surpass 10 billion and experience even greater income inequality. According to PWC, the global economy is expected to grow by 150% by 2050, with China rising to 20% share of the world's GDP in purchasing power parity, India surpassing the United States, reducing the EU's GDP share below 10%. Indeed, economic historians such as Paul Kennedy have also observed that such prognostications of a radical shift in global economic power are especially distressing given the implications for the least economically advantaged regions of the world, such as Africa, developing Asia and the Middle East where renewable resources are ever increasingly scarce and climate change and the unabated growth of indigenous arms capabilities is sharpening the divisions that emerge from ethnic conflict and economic desperation.

● The Decline of Economic Globalization

In this unstable context, the four pillars of economic globalization – **production, finance, information, and talent** – are crumbling. With respect to production, the degree of integration of global value chains (GVC) continues its decline since 2008 and the U.S. has also adopted the highest tariffs in its recorded history. Meanwhile, several countries are establishing alternative reserve currencies, China-based companies have opted for secondary listings in Hong Kong and Saudi Aramco, the largest IPO ever at $25.6 billion dollars is listed on the Tadawul stock exchange.

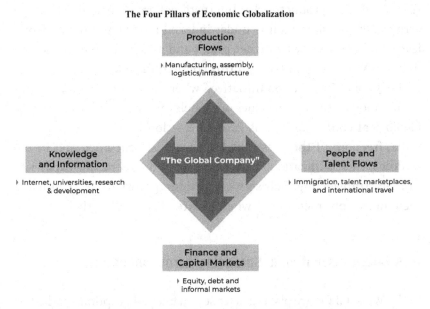

Figure 1.1: The four pillars of economic globalization

● A decline in global talent and information flows has huge implications for Western countries

Information flows are also suffering with the rise of digital firewalls, including internet infrastructure, social media as well as cloud and data storage. LinkedIn's once global professional community has exited China after 30 years of investment due to increasing regulatory costs, greater censorship, and data controls. This leaves Chinese talents in the world's largest service economy of 70 million people without a professional networking platform to showcase their skills, network with peers or seek employment in international companies.

Around the world, people flows, including legal immigration of skilled talent, are facing severe bottlenecks. Brexit has exacerbated labor shortages in the U.K. in critical sectors such as healthcare and cybersecurity, the waiting period for a U.S. visa is over 500 days for Indian travelers, and the massive backlog of H1B Visa applications risks slowing AI product cycles. International travel, including Chinese arrivals, is also significantly under-indexed relative to pre-pandemic levels and is set back by higher prices and a lack of feeling welcome in many Western countries. In this context, President Xi's unveiling of the "Global Civilization Initiative," where countries "should refrain from imposing their own values or models on others and from stoking ideological confrontation," is gaining traction in foreign capitals. In India, freedom of the press has been seriously curtailed and in the Middle East, "Saudization," bans employers from recruiting expatriate workers, transferring their services, assigning work to them, or using them in the jobs mentioned, whether directly or indirectly.

• A Talent Disruption is Spreading Across Industries

In the West, CEOs are playing defense as a talent disruption, marked by the parallel rise of the gig economy and unionization, is crippling entire service industries with labor strikes from hospitality and entertainment to healthcare and commercial real estate that placed bets on the return of a traditional labor model post-pandemic. However, a vast undersupply of 5 million highly skilled trapped talents exists in markets such as China, Russia, Iran, Pakistan, Bangladesh, and India that can use AI to transform industries and create entirely new ones. The decisions CEOs make in the coming years regarding the talent supply chain will determine which countries and industries capture talent and whether the free movement of people can be rescued for future generations.

Many corporate executives, boards of directors and institutional investors don't get it. In public they say all the right things: people are our most important asset, investing in human capital is key to our future. But privately they believe "the labor problem" will fix itself with one time pay raises, a larger dose of employer brand marketing and worse case, an economic recession. Boards of directors are also suffering from fatigue after rolling out years of environmental social and governance (ESG) and diversity, equity, and inclusion (DEI) related initiatives, including new disclosures, targets and scorecards.

It turns out, the "E" in ESG should have been for employees.

Some visionary HR leaders are experimenting with AI tech solutions with millions of employees in financial services, healthcare, and consumer industries. The biggest challenge organizations face is not cybersecurity. It's overcoming orthodoxies about who the best talents are, who should be promoted and how they should be compensated.

Despite growing questions from the investment community, few CEOs debate the root causes of the labor strife with their management teams prior to threats of unionization or strikes. Even fewer understand their HR tech stack and how big HR technologies control the talent markets and know more about their employees than they do. Now unions and gig apps like Uber and DoorDash are driving a large, fast-moving truck into this blind spot.

A talent disruption is when parents save up money for kids' college education and they decide to earn a living by becoming influencers on social media and driving an Uber part time. Unemployment rates return extremely low despite historically high interest rates because 50 million Americans are freelancing and working multiple jobs, including remotely. Their ultimate dream is to build their personal brand and have the flexibility to live their life their own way. As more industries get disrupted by their employees, they also become more vulnerable to new competition.

An industry or business is experiencing talent disruption if unit labor economics have grown 20% over 3 years and it has lost 20% share of its elite talent (top 10%). Even after factoring in less turnover due to a recession and recapturing talents lost to other industries, the U.S. hotel industry will have a gap of 2.4 million talents required to meet pent up demand. An extension of temporary worker visas by an additional 100,000 will not have significant impact.

The symptoms of talent disruption include historic income inequality, persistent DEI gaps and growing tensions between employers and talents over remote work. The root cause is mismanagement and a lack of meritocracy. Internal bureaucracies and fiefdoms are severely limiting free market enterprise opportunities for the front-line. For example, actors not being paid fair residuals for AI replacements; or hotel workers not being paid a share of the profits after a sale or refinancing. These management failures are resulting in growing unionization, more government regulations and labor strikes costing billions of dollars a week.

Big tech platforms are an unhealthy addiction that is clogging the arteries. Studies have found that applicant tracking systems filter out 80% of semi-qualified applicants such as those out of the workforce for a year. Research proves that women and minorities don't apply to jobs if they don't check all the boxes. A more strategic problem with Big HR tech is that they hoard data and enable both incorrect and fake employer reviews.

Some people fear that AI will increase inequality and displace millions of workers, such as actors, truck drivers and even doctors. Many people are anxious that AI will take over their lives and livelihoods, but is it really a problem if AI manages tasks such as cleaning the bathroom, making beds, and sweeping floors? These are laborious tasks that no human being finds enjoyable, regardless of their background and social class. Decent work is a human right. Human beings are social and political beings who seek dignity, recognition, reciprocity, association, and security. These fundamental needs cannot be met by labor intensive jobs, poor compensation, and exploitative contracts.

Employers, on the other hand, face many challenges in improving their profits as the labor costs are extremely high due to high turnover rate, high taxes, and labor shortage. These factors make it difficult for them to improve the quality of their workforce and increase their pay. However, there are two things that can benefit both workers and employers: AI and automation.

AI and automation offer significant benefits for both employers and employees. For businesses, these technologies can reduce labor costs, boost productivity, and sharpen competitive edges. Workers, on the other hand, can be relieved of monotonous, repetitive tasks, enabling them to concentrate on more creative and fulfilling work. Additionally, these advancements open up new avenues for learning and professional development. AI and automation are not threats to workers and employers, but rather tools for mutual benefit and cooperation.

● Key Strategic Opportunities in an Unstable Multi-Polar World

In the coming years, Western CEOs have a unique opportunity to capitalize on global instability by building talent marketplaces, with supply chains that attract a disproportionate share of highly skilled, elite talent pools in artificial intelligence, data science and climate technologies. A turnaround starts with measuring human capital and recording it on the balance sheet. KPIs include quality of talent, benchmarked against competitive sets. CEOs need to look at this, as well as financial and customer data every day.

In many industries whose factories have been financially engineered by short-term investors - like hospitals and hotels - the traditional labor model is not economically sustainable. For example, there's a forecasted shortage of 500,000 nurses and doctors in the U.S. with out-of-control contract labor costs. However, AI, telemedicine and virtual diagnostics are rationalizing its cost structure and empowering its workforce.

Thanks to AI, there's an opportunity to change the game. In sports, the Moneyball movement used data science to source undervalued players and build winning teams with modest budgets. Similarly, meritocracy requires implementing AI driven marketplaces that place a value on talents, predict career paths and enable mobility. AI can also offer learning and development and give people a nudge as needed.

To achieve this end, CEOs should set three strategic priorities over the next five years to balance creating shareholder value in the short term with the long-term interests of key stakeholders. The first opportunity is to import 2 million highly skilled AI-ready talents from distressed labor markets, such as China where youth unemployment is above 20% to secondary or allied markets such as Australia, New

Zealand, and Canada, who are facing long-term labor shortages and could be springboards to the U.S. Unfortunately, the building blocks employed by most companies today are deeply flawed: legacy HR technologies including applicant tracking systems and job sites are exacerbating labor shortages. A comprehensive study by Harvard Business School and Accenture found that over 27 million "Hidden Workers," including those with employment gaps of more than 6 months, immigrants, caregivers, relocating partners and spouses, veterans, and those with physical disabilities, were excluded from consideration by existing HR technologies in the U.S. Hence, the process begins with CEOs investing resources to build AI-driven global talent marketplaces that identify, and source rising talents from distressed markets and use augmented and virtual reality to offer experiential learning and development capabilities that convert analysts into managers faster and cheaper than ever imagined.

The second opportunity is to gain talent share, build brands with a purpose that serve as global citizens and employers of choice. The process starts with a new paradigm for human capital management rooted in open talent marketplaces where vetted talents join a network of like-minded employers. For example, Hilton could work with its franchisees, Starbucks, and Mayo clinic to enable culinary and restaurant management talent to be ranked, put into tiers, priced, and moved between like-minded organizations. In franchised businesses such as hospitality, owners and franchisees can lead the way by pushing profit sharing down to the front-line. They can partner with AI experts to use inexpensive applications that source talent off the beaten path. This includes experimenting with floating wages that reflect supply and demand like gig apps in hospitals that use yield management to determine wages for nurses. Rather than trying to enforce non-competition clauses, franchisees can also build shared talent networks with each other to reduce their costs, partnering with local organizations.

The third opportunity is to restructure their talent supply chains to capitalize on the new geopolitical fault lines. The UNHCR estimates the total number of people worldwide who were forced to flee their homes due to conflicts, violence, fear of persecution and human rights violations ("displaced people"), surpassed 100 million in 2022, of which 22 million were classified as refugees, a 200% increase from a decade earlier. CEOs can start by establishing talent safe havens that protect the rights of women, minorities, and displaced people and by pooling resources with stakeholders and non-profits. The long-term goal should be to pool resources to sponsor highly skilled employees and their families in alignment with NGOs to manage logistics of moving people across borders.

As relationships between Washington D.C., London, Beijing, New Delhi, San Paulo and the GCC become more tempestuous, governments will introduce new regulations to trap skilled workers and wall off data. In the process, new growth opportunities will also emerge from the chaos as regional talent alliances are formed between civilizations – for example, between the West, India, Japan, South Korea, and Vietnam on one hand and between China, Russia and the GCC, on the other. In conclusion, it is critical for leaders to understand that the forces that are fomenting a global talent disruption are here now, and no industry is immune. The decisions CEOs make in the coming year will determine whether we win the AI arms race and preserve global talent flows for future generations.

"The best CEOs I know are teachers, and at the core of what they teach is strategy."

Michael Porter

2

BEYOND THE GOLDEN
AGE OF TRAVEL

According to the renowned scholars C.K. Prahalad and Gary Hamel, authors of the classic *Competing for the Future* and developers of the thesis of "core competence," a corporate strategy is composed of a strategic intent ("rallying cry") and a strategic architecture ("the three or four dimensions of competition a company will be known for"). The dimensions of a strategic architecture are by definition unique to a company and reflect management's perspective on the discontinuities in technology and society that shape the future and their innovation domains or clusters of activities that challenge the status quo and overturn industry orthodoxies. The strategic architecture provides a blueprint with milestones, the most significant of which reflect hallmark achievements of the company. Strategic architecture is a reflection not just of a company's one or two current core competencies (defined by a unique combination of skills, processes, technologies, values and assets), but also future investments required to build new core competencies to achieve a strategic intent.

However, in mature and commoditizing industries, management teams often fail to rally stakeholders and are left to compete on the same dimensions of an outdated strategic architecture. In other words, they lack a strategy and often take their cue from the same community of management consultants, bankers, trade organizations, attorneys, media and public relations firms. Eventually, the industry consolidates around a few players and new entrants emerge to displace incumbents.

Just as reading a country's constitution would not convey whether its form of governance is democratic or authoritarian, a company's strategy is not usually discovered by reading annual reports, corporate press releases and communications, advertising and social media posts. The best way to uncover a company's strategy is to objectively analyze the DNA of its management team, the organization chart to see where the highest paid people and teams reside, its capital investments and above all how the senior management team spends its time. In the 2020s hotel and accommodations sector, corporate strategies have converged in a commoditization process with industry incumbents executing near identical strategies, in a race to the bottom.

● Historical Context for Strategy in the Hospitality Sector

Thanks to the DNA of its board and C-Suite, the hospitality industry has become a "high finance" real estate business. From quick service restaurant chains such as McDonald's to coffee shops such as Starbucks who own and lease billions of dollars in real estate on one end of the spectrum to single asset billion-dollar branded resorts, timeshares, and residences such as Ritz Carlton on the other, the industry uses high amounts of debt, including from non-traditional sources and cutting edge financial engineering innovations to monetize assets and create wealth for equity and debt investors.

The game differs by geography but remains a real estate business at its core. In the U.S., hotels can be highly leveraged up to 70 percent or greater with various tranches of collateralized and securitized debt. Usually, the bet pays off as hotels generate huge cyclical cash flows and benefit from real estate appreciation. For example, the U.S. hotel industry experienced 12 consecutive years of record operating profits over $80 billion prior to 2020. In other regions of the world, particularly in China, metropolitan hotels may be largely unprofitable; however, incorporating 5-star hotel brands into development projects can offer ancillary benefits to developers, such as obtaining government permits, securing access to government-supported bank loans, and boosting residential, commercial, and retail rental rates by 30 to 40 percent.

● Creating shareholder value

Despite progressive talk about ESG, the primary governing objective of U.S. based corporations, including hospitality chains, is to create shareholder value. Since 2018, the lion's share of the equity market capitalization has been captured by search engines and online travel agencies (OTAs), led by Google Travel, Airbnb, and Booking.com. As of March 31st, 2023, Booking.com's equity market capitalization is more than that of the three biggest U.S. based hotel chains (Marriott, Hilton, and Wyndham) combined (see figure 2.1). This suggests that the market ascribes a far greater value to agnostic technology platforms despite their lack of inventory ownership, established loyalty programs, and management capabilities that enable hotels to generate 30 to 50 percent additional revenue streams.

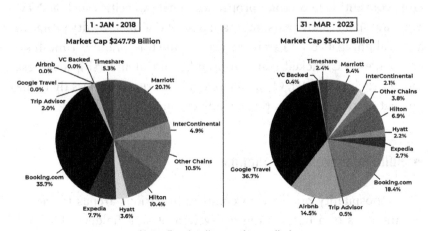

Note: For details, see Appendix I.

Figure 2.1: Value migration in hotels and online travel

Furthermore, despite decades of mergers and acquisitions and unprecedented brand growth, there is no clear-cut winner among global hotel chains. The top 5 global hotel chains – Marriott, Hilton, Accor, IHG, and Wyndham – collectively account for 21 percent of equity market capitalization. Marriott, the largest global hotel chain by number of properties, leads the race with 9.4 percent of total value created and trades in line with its peers. However, Hilton, which grew its market cap by 46 percent versus only three percent for Marriott in the same 5-year period (2018 through 2023), represents only 6.9 percent of the economic pie.

The economic rationale for the gap in trading multiples between the two rivals is that Hilton generates over 70 percent of its revenues from franchising less economically sensitive limited-service hotels primarily in the U.S., while Marriott generates the majority of its fees through more cyclical management and incentive fees from full-service hotels with greater exposure to international markets such as China. Another interesting difference between the two is that in the 15-year period between 2008 to 2023, Hilton grew organically by adding limited-service and economy franchised brands without acquiring any other brands or companies and divested its relatively capital intensive timeshare business. In contrast, Marriott acquired Starwood, whose focus was operating high end union hotels, including large convention and group properties in gateway cities such as New York and spent many years integrating its operations, loyalty program and realigning its brand architecture. Meanwhile, branded timeshare companies, VC backed start-up brands, and membership business models such as Sonder, Oyo, and Soho House represent less than one percent of total equity market capitalization.

● Building stakeholder alignment

Today, hospitality brands also compete in various arenas to satisfy the interests of a burgeoning ecosystem of stakeholders. The five major stakeholders include equity shareholders, hotel owners and lenders, state, county, and city governments, individual and group customers, and talent, including employees and contracted labor. At the intersection of this ecosystem of stakeholders, each of whom has its own food chains, there is the ultimate long-term objective: building brand equity. To succeed, these brands must generate economic profits via returns on invested capital that exceed their weighted average cost of capital for their shareholders, achieve millions of dollars in lifetime customer value for their highest worth individual and group customers, and garner and sustain a disproportionate share of elite talent (see figure 2.2).

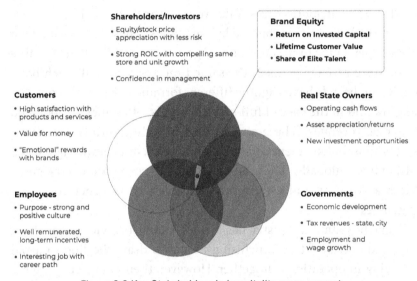

Shareholders/Investors
- Equity/stock price appreciation with less risk
- Strong ROIC with compelling same store and unit growth
- Confidence in management

Brand Equity:
- **Return on Invested Capital**
- **Lifetime Customer Value**
- **Share of Elite Talent**

Customers
- High satisfaction with products and services
- Value for money
- "Emotional" rewards with brands

Real State Owners
- Operating cash flows
- Asset appreciation/returns
- New investment opportunities

Employees
- Purpose - strong and positive culture
- Well remunerated, long-term incentives
- Interesting job with career path

Governments
- Economic development
- Tax revenues - state, city
- Employment and wage growth

Figure 2.2 Key Stakeholders in hospitality management

These stakeholders include state, county, city governments, and tourism improvement districts whose interests are to build the brand equity of their respective jurisdictions as travel destinations. These government entities levy occupancy taxes of five percent to 20 percent of rooms revenue typically for transient stays under 30 days. These taxes on room revenues are expected to generate a record $46 billion windfall in tax revenue in 2023, up 13 percent from the pre-pandemic peak year of 2019. Additional stakeholders include long-term technology vendors, such as property management systems and revenue management software, who are incorporated in brand standards and supported by consulting firms that implement solutions that perpetuate dependence on their software developers, contact centers and methods to provide cybersecurity.

● Hotel brand fees and the franchise model

Hotel taxes pale in comparison to the 15 percent to 20 percent of ongoing revenue franchise fees, including royalties, advertising or marketing contribution fees, sales/reservation/loyalty program fees, and miscellaneous fees charged by the brands. These fees have grown at eight percent compounded annual growth since 2013, far exceeding same store revenue gains in the same time period. While each hotel chain and brands have slightly different formulas, these fees continue to grow and in the case of full-service brands, often include food and beverage revenues. These annual fees, including loyalty programs, soft brands, independent collections, and residential branding, exceed $120 billion globally. These funds cover the corporate overheads of the brand teams and loyalty programs, as well as other corporate initiatives.

The hospitality industry has formed a universal viewpoint about the boundaries of the franchising model to draw the line to avoid engaging in operations altogether. However, their contracts preserve a great deal of flexibility. Ironically, while owners' councils may review the allocation of funds, Uniform Franchise Offering Circulars (UFOCs) provide brands with extremely broad discretion in how they are used. Historically, brands have steered clear of using their funds to support franchisees in any human capital related matters, such as recruiting, learning and development, performance reviews, compensation practices, work rules, diversity, equity and inclusion often citing potential legal liabilities as the reason to draw this line. MogulRecruiter's survey of 100 UFOC agreements found an average of only two paragraphs in a 200-page agreement dedicated to human capital management - a few scant references to half-day mandatory General Manager and Assistant General Manager training in brand standards. With respect to architectural and design brand standards, our research across 100 brands and surveys with owners found few guidelines addressing the "back of the house," or "heart of the house" as some luxury brands call dedicated employee workplaces, with no minimum requirements for lockers, cafeterias, or even employee entrances.

However, there is a significant possibility that new government regulations will "blow up" the traditional franchising model in hospitality. As this book is being written, the Biden Administration is attempting to enact new policies reflected in the National Labor Relations Board (NLRB) that it go into effect Dec. 26, 2023 stating that "an entity may be considered a joint employer of a group of employees if each entity has an employment relationship with the employees and they share or co-determine one or more of the employees' essential terms and conditions of employment." In a news release, the American Hotel Lodging Association (AHLA) said it has filed suit along with the U.S. Chamber of Commerce and other plaintiffs with the U.S. District Court for the Eastern District of Texas to challenge the legality of the National Labor Relations Board's new final rule on determining when two companies could be considered joint employers of workers. The new standard will change the liability exposures for businesses such as hotel brands, owners and management companies that work together. More specifically for the hotel industry, it will create joint liabilities impacting the roles and relationships between hotel franchisors and franchisees, hotel owners and third-party managers, and hotel operators and staffing agencies, among others. In turn, this would put the onus back on the hotel chains to play a more active role in human resources, including recruiting, training and compliance.

Nevertheless, the U.S. capital markets have memorialized the value of asset-light franchising, valuing hospitality brands inversely to their capital and management intensity. For the trailing 12 months ending April 2023, publicly traded hotel chains created $760 million of economic value with a weighted average ROIC of 11.5 percent.

The largest valuations are ascribed to high growth, franchise-driven, global brands at 12-15X EBITDA such as those of Hilton and Marriott whose returns on invested capital (ROIC) exceed their cost of capital during most of the industry cycle. At the other end of the spectrum, asset heavy hotel chains such as Hyatt and Accor failed to create economic value during much of the last industry cycle. Except for Host Hotels and Ryman, hotel REITS (which own real estate, not brands) also struggled to typically generate attractive yields or create economic value. None of the third party management companies that manage properties without their own brands have been publicly traded since Interstate hotels, which was acquired by Aimbridge Hospitality. During its tenure as a publicly traded management company that did not own any brands, Interstate, a pure management company, traded between 5-8X EBITDA, well below that of hotel chains and more in line with REITS. Holding all factors equal, the market also ascribes two to three basis points higher EBITDA multiples to franchise driven brands with high ROICs and internally managed lifestyle and luxury brands on the other hand, which command long-term contracts 25 years or longer and have residential branding fees of five to 10 percent of revenue - a proxy for the value they create for real estate developers. Hence, when it was publicly traded, Four Seasons hotels had a multiple of 25-40X EBITDA (or greater with frequent negative earnings when it was publicly traded) and many relatively small luxury brands sold for 15-20X EBITDA despite having a relatively small footprint (see table 2.1).

However, the valuations of hotel chains pale in comparison to the category leading online travel agencies such as Booking.com and Airbnb, which created over $10 billion of economic value with ROICs ranging from 30 percent to 94 percent during the same period.

Managed/Franchised

Company	Ticker Symbol	ROIC	Value Creation ($M)	TEV/ EBITDA	Market Cap. ($M)	Weight	% of Profit from Hotels Owned/Leased
Marriott	MAR	10.5%	$387	15.0x	$51,287	42%	8%
InterContinental	IHG	17.6%	$107	19.1x	$11,707	10%	3%
Wyndham	WH	9.8%	$89	13.2x	$5,849	5%	0%
Choice	CHH	28.8%	$315	13.6x	$5,982	5%	0%
Hilton	HLT	10.6%	$289	19.2x	$37,535	31%	4%
Accor	AC.PA	1.8%	($427)	16.5x	$8,447	7%	20%
Weighted Average		11.5%	$760	16.6x	$120,808	100%	

Owned/Leased

Company	Ticker Symbol	ROIC	Value Creation ($M)	TEV/ EBITDA	Market Cap. ($M)	% of Adj. EBITDA from Hotels Owned/Leased
Hyatt	H	2.5%	($368)	16.2x	$11,878	34%

OTA

Company	Ticker Symbol	ROIC	Value Creation ($M)	TEV / EBITDA	Market Cap. ($M)	Weight	Price / Book (Current)
Expedia	EXPE	4.3%	($283)	13.3x	$14,879	8%	7.1x
Booking.com	BKNG	31.5%	$3,841	17.6x	$99,859	51%	29.2x
TripAdvisor	TRIP	-0.3%	($136)	19.5x	$2,800	1%	3.6x
AirBnb	ABNB	94.4%	$6,844	36.9x	$78,537	40%	13.0x
Total / Weighted Average		54.2%	$10,266	25.0x	$196,075	100%	20.7x

REITs

Company	Ticker Symbol	OCF / IC Yield	Value Creation ($M)	TEV / EBITDA	Market Cap. ($M)	Weight	Price / Book (Current)
Ryman Hospitality	RHP	12.4%	$197	12.8x	$4,892	19%	74.9x
HOST	HST	12.5%	$675	10.3x	$11,765	45%	1.8x
Apple Hospitality REIT	APLE	8.1%	$71	11.8x	$3,560	14%	1.2x
Park	PK	5.1%	($70)	10.4x	$2,743	10%	0.7x
Xenia	XHR	6.4%	$4	10.0x	$1,459	6%	1.1x
Pebblebrook Hotel Trust	PEB	4.9%	($66)	13.1x	$1,769	7%	0.6x
Weighted Average		10.3%	$811	11.2x	$26,188	100%	

Table 2.1 Valuation of global hotel chains and OTAs - March 2023

Given the brutal efficiency of the capital markets that ascribes more value to franchising, and the ever shrinking holding periods of U.S. stock market or public market equity investors to under a year, it's not surprising that hospitality executives, whose long-term compensation is tied to share price performance, are predisposed to franchising rather than managing operations, with minimal investments in technology innovation. Hence, hotel franchising has witnessed explosive growth with 3,000 new properties added to its business model from 2017 to 2022 and six out of seven employees work for franchisees as opposed to brands, the opposite ratio that existed in 1995. The franchising business model continues to experience double-digit growth in both the U.S. and China despite the absence of effective intellectual property protections and dispute resolution mechanisms for international brands (see figure 2.3).

Growth Of Franchising Model In U.S. And China

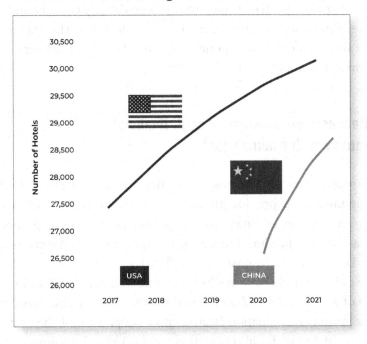

Source: FRANdata 2020, the companies, Statista
Figure 2.3 Growth of franchising business model Since 2017

● Downside of franchising: brand dilution

While hotel brands and operators like to say their greatest asset is their talent, evidence suggests investments in people and HR processes are usually addressed on a leftover basis as needed, typically in the context of property or corporate mergers and acquisitions.

The contradiction is that franchising has not been proven to work at the high end of the business, with only a few exceptions in the highest growth international markets. Research performed by numerous independent consulting firms and internally by several hotel and restaurant chains demonstrates that an employee's engagement is greatly impacted by the General Manager (r2=35 percent) and the culture of the management company (r2=20 percent) far above real estate factors such as product quality (r2=12 percent) and location (r2=15 percent). But if the research about these interdependencies is so clear, why couldn't the brands adjust their business model to help their operators protect their brands? Put differently, how did real estate owners and lenders extract record profits at the expense of other stakeholders, sending one of the world's biggest industries into a commoditization cycle?

● Real estate/management split: financial returns with a human cost

A corporate strategy for hospitality firms must address real estate development and provide guidelines for the target mix of owned, joint venture, leased, managed, franchised and licensed properties for each brand, product line and geographic market. Americans are familiar with the blockbuster movie hit, *The Founder*, which tells the story of how a milkshake machine salesman named Ray Kroc became CEO of McDonald's and built a real estate company that earns most of its profits and valuation from owning 45 percent of the land and 70 percent of the buildings at their 36,000 plus locations. Former McDonald's CFO Harry J. Sonneborn said, "We are not technically in the food business. We are in the real estate business. The only reason we sell fifteen-cent hamburgers is because they are the greatest producer of revenue from which our tenants can pay us our rent." This is reminiscent of the U.S. hotel industry, which started with an asset-heavy business model that attracted real estate developers. For example, in the 1990s, Hilton owned over 200 hotels in the U.S. and made one-third to half its income during economic boom periods from recapitalizations, refinancing, and financial engineering. As recently as 2005, Marriott had billions of dollars of balance sheet debt, with the most complex financial statements and disclosures of any Fortune 500 company at the time. The upshot was they also invested in hospitality schools, managed most or all their full-service hotels, and even leveraged their HR infrastructure and brands to manage assisted living facilities, timeshares, and casino resorts. Hotel brands were winning awards for service quality across sectors and employees knew who they worked for and how they could build a rising and relatively stable career.

This changed in the late 1990s and 2000s. Financial engineers led by former Marriott and Disney CFO Steve Bollenbach (who later became Hilton CEO for over a decade and whose administration I worked in for three years as head of corporate development), capitalized on market inefficiencies and spun out hotel real estate into tax efficient REITs starting with Marriott. Marriott later split into Host Hotels, the largest hotel REIT, and Marriott International, the largest hotel chain, and later Marriott divested its assisted living and vacation ownership businesses. At the time, Marriott mostly managed hotels and had just started scaling the franchising of the one-time category killer Courtyard by Marriott. This "prop-co/op-co split" caught on and hotel chains adjusted their strategic architectures to be "asset right," which required owning a select number of the valuable real estate assets in the most attractive market at the right time, including balancing cities and resorts and creating an optimal portfolio that included non-cyclical or countercyclical cash flows optimal. In the context of this industry transformation, hotel REITs were eclipsed by private equity, family office and sovereign real estate funds and dedicated hotel equity and debt funds became highly specialized by investment stage, hotel segment, product type, and by market and geography. By 2019, private equity, in its various forms, increased its ownership of U.S. hotel rooms to 59 percent, up from only 12 percent in 2003 while REITs dropped from 67 percent to only 33 percent. High net worth individuals, including family offices, account for the majority of the remaining hotel investors, six percent of ownership in 2019, with the remaining two percent represented by cities, sovereign funds and state-owned enterprises such as those based in the GCC, Singapore and China.

Evolution of Hotel Ownership in the U.S. 2003-2019

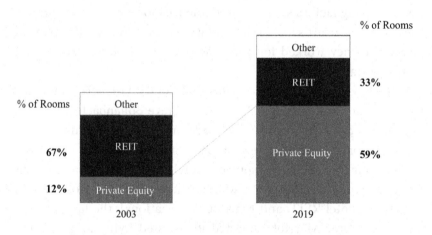

Figure 2.4 Evolution of hotel ownership in the U.S. 2003-2019

Therefore, unlike McDonald's and Starbucks, who play the checkers version of a real estate game, hotel investing is a more strategic game of chess that is difficult to predict precisely and model. As a trading business, hotel investment is often a full-blown drama resembling a home flipping reality television show as new owners come and go on average every 5.5 years. To maximize real estate investor returns and ensure assets are unencumbered, most owners do their best to separate the brands from less expensive and more flexible management companies, who are themselves put on a short leash with an average of 90-day termination rights, sometimes as short as 30 days. The drama unfolds as owners, led by private equity firms, who can profit handsomely on both sides of the business cycle by minimizing equity investments, converting senior, junior debt and mezzanine loans to equity, borrowing from banks to reposition assets, leasing unprofitable restaurants, spas and other services to improve margins, extracting union concessions wherever possible, and if necessary, changing management companies and brands or even creating new brands of their own.

● Hotel chains: doubling down on opportunism

Hotel brands have also adjusted their tactics to create value for their shareholders and ensure their survival in the real estate game. As the industry evolved through mergers and acquisitions, a short-term mindset prevailed as brands adopted highly complex business models by owning hotels that were cash cows, managing most high-end properties, and widely franchising both upscale and limited-service hotels. Over time, brands deteriorated due to inconsistency and lack of brand standards enforcement, and the mix of owned, managed and franchised business models became ripe with potential conflicts of interest. This also started creating internal "turf wars" inside hotel chains where the same teams fought over deals. For example, brand teams who preferred to scale through franchising and third-party management came into direct conflict with the executives of their own management company as hotel chain operators sought to sustain their relevance to the real estate capital markets. Furthermore, inside asset-heavy hotel chains, real estate and asset management teams sought to monetize underutilized assets and refinance and recycle hotel investments based on their "privileged insights" rather than invest small amounts of equity, debt, or key money to buy management or franchising deals. The few full-service brands that achieved stakeholder alignment and consistently enabled revenue premiums and higher fees – for example Westin, which became a category killer in the upper upscale segment, charged owners three percent to five percent of revenue more than its peers – did so by masterfully managing a portfolio of owned and managed hotels churning over 50 percent in less than a decade. Other brands such as Sheraton, Crowne Plaza, Howard Johnson, DoubleTree, and Holiday Inn became tired, inconsistent, and lost relevance with consumers and employees.

● When all else fails, create new brands

As upscale or full-service hotel assets age and go through renovations, whether new build or conversion, they become dissimilar to the consumer, which creates another play: reflagging into another brand. But this ideal outcome is unusual – most of the time, owners and lenders forgo this risk. Over the past decade, U.S. hotel owners have funded at least $1 billion of new televisions, beds and replaced bathtubs with shower only bathrooms using the same furniture, fixtures, architects and designers. It's extremely rare for a hotel to be removed from the system of a hotel chain altogether, no matter how poorly it performed. What's even more rare – unlike other consumer-facing industries such as packaged goods or automobiles (In 2004, Oldsmobile, a 106-year-old automobile brand, was retired by General Motors) – is the elimination of a hotel brand due to poor performance or redundant characteristics.

Hotel brands have almost never been phased out even when a similar brand was acquired or developed. The complication for hotel chains has become a consistently incoherent portfolio, where a lower-priced brand with fewer services often can have a superior offering in a certain market and charge more than a higher-end brand which may only be a few decades old. Over time, this discrepancy undermines direct bookings and drives up marketing and cost of sales as consumers flock to meta review sites and online travel agencies such as Booking.com, Expedia, and TripAdvisor for impartial and timely information on their purchase decisions rather than relying on the brand's reputation to tell them what to expect.

Instead of prudently managing a portfolio of brands like other consumer businesses, hotel chains have risked cannibalization by introducing new brands, attempting to create micro-segments similar to what Toyota has done in the automobile business with over 35 brands. Multi-unit hotel chains created over 120 new brands between 2003 and 2018 (see figure 2.5).

Growth in Number of Global Hotel Brands

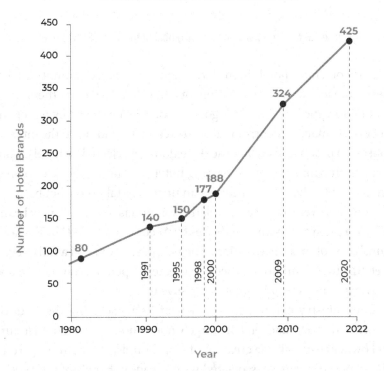

Figure 2.5 Growth in number of global hotel brands
Source: Bear Steams 2001, STR 2001, PriceWaterHouse Coopers 2001, American Hotel and Lodging Association, 2001. (M&A's-Mergers and Acquisition)

During the same period, the five major U.S. hotel chains increased their brand portfolios by 35 percent through a combination of organic development and acquisitions. Mergers and acquisitions have further compounded the issue of brand portfolios that lack consistency and coherence (see figure 2.6).

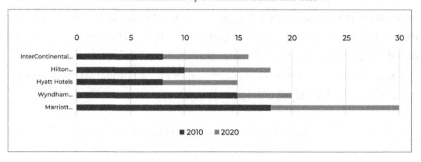

Figure 2.6 New brands launched by global hotel chains 2010-2020

In theory, most hotel chains have capital or finance committees that assess "impact," or cannibalization, of a new hotel against others when deciding to approve whether it goes forward as proposed by either the franchising, management, or real estate team, depending on the internal sponsor. In practice, franchise deals seldom get rejected by hotel chains due to cannibalization of its existing hotels, including the ones owned or managed by the chain. If there's an uncomfortable conflict between hotel owners over the same brand, the solution is to create a new brand extension (such as Ibis and Ibis Styles by Accor), a co-brand "by the hotel chain," or a soft brand affiliation. The net present value of a full-service hotel, $15 to $25 millions in fees or greater depending on its size and brand segment, is simply too good to give up.

The industry extended the reach of its franchising distribution platform to attract independent, largely non-union, boutique and luxury hotel owners through the creation of "soft brands," a long-term pattern in hotel branding often associated with "Leading Hotels of the World" and started in chains by Starwood's luxury collection – an affiliation network of distinctive luxury boutique properties that leverage the chains' booking engine, reward program and other sales platforms.

The bigger issue is that the brand portfolios of the hotel chains no longer make sense to consumers because their features and services are not aligned with their relative prices. Few consumers can tell most brands apart or describe their distinctive features, let alone soft brand collections. As a case in point, we examined the 14 hotel choices on www.marriott.com for a 3-star to 5-star hotel 2-night stay in Times Square, New York on weekdays in April 2023. What's striking is that the average daily rates are actually higher for the 3-star tier, limited-service branded hotels such as Courtyard, Fairfield, and Four Points than most full-service brands such as Westin, W, Renaissance, and Marriott. Even the full-service Sheraton brand is priced less than its limited-service spin-off, Four Points by Sheraton. To be fair, these higher priced limited-service hotels are relatively new, opening over the past seven years or earlier, but they offer fewer amenities and lower service levels (see Figure 2.7).

Marriott Branded Hotels in Times Square NYC

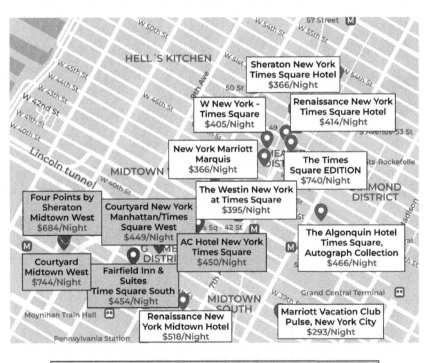

Limited service opened after 2013 (100% franchised)

Full service (20% franchised)

Figure 2.7 Marriott branded hotels in Times Square NYC

Furthermore, when we analyze the ownership and management of these 14 hotels – facts that are not disclosed to consumers on any website, not even review sites or online travel agencies – there are nine different management companies and 12 different owners. Regarding the limited-service hotels, each one has a different owner, and three are owner-operated (see table 2.2).

Marriott Midtown Manhattan- Full-Service Hotels

Property	Management Company	Owner	Address	Nightly Rate	Stars	Year Opened
The Algonquin Hotel Times Square	HEI Hotels & Resorts	Cornerstone Real Estate Advisors	59 West 44th Street	$466	4	1902
W New York - Times Square	Marriott International	Marriott International	1567 Broadway	$405	4	2001
New York Marriott Marquis	Marriott International	Host Hotels & Resorts	1535 Broadway	$366	4	1985
Renaissance New York Times Square Hotel	Marriott International	Marriott International	714 Seventh Avenue	$414	4	1992
Marriott Vacation Club Pulse, New York City	Marriott Vacation Ownership	Marriott Vacation Ownership	33 West 37th Street	$293	4	2009
The Westin New York at Times Square	Marriott International	Tishman Realty and Construction	270 West 43rd Street	$395	4	2002
Renaissance New York Midtown Hotel	Marriott International	Stonebridge Companies	218 West 35th Street	$518	4	2015
Sheraton New York Times Square Hotel	MCR Hotels	MCR Hotels & Island Capital Group	811 7th Avenue 53rd Street	$366	4	1962
The Times Square EDITION	Marriott International	Natixis	701 7th Avenue	$740	5	2021

Marriott Midtown Manhattan- Limited-Service Hotels

Property	Management Company	Owner	Address	Nightly Rate	Stars	Year Opened
AC Hotel New York Times Square	OTO Development, LLC	OTO Development	260 West 40th Street	$450	4	2018
Courtyard New York Manhattan/Midtown West	Endeavor Hospitality Group	Endeavor Hospitality Group	461 West 34th Street	$744	3	2019
Courtyard New York Manhattan/Times Square West	Stonebridge Companies	Stonebridge Companies	307 West 37th Street	$449	3	2013
Fairfield Inn & Suites / Times Square South	Real Hospitality Group	Gehr Group	338 West 36th Street	$454	4	2019
Four Points by Sheraton - Midtown West	Real Hospitality Group	Joy Construction	444 10th Avenue	$684	4	2016

Source: Marriott.com

Table 2.2 Ownership and management of Marriott hotels in Times Square NYC

Marriott manages 5 of the full-service hotels that are unionized and owns two of them outright. While all employees wear Marriott uniforms, only the managed hotels receive human capital related services from Marriott, including recruiting, training, development, and career paths. In other words, Marriott's own management company may compete with its franchisees for talent. Rather than franchise territories like other businesses do, it has created an ecosystem where multiple owners and management companies compete for the same customer and talent pool. This is not an uncommon predicament isolated to New York – the highly fragmented ownership and management of hotels, the inconsistency of brands and potential conflicts of interest can be found in all major markets for hotel chains across the country.

● Conclusion

Performance in the labor, consumer and capital markets confirms that leading global hospitality chains are absent a strategic intent ("rallying cry"). Their strategic architectures are converging to deliver the same benefits to hotel owners and consumers through franchising, contract labor and outsourcing management, reward programs and online distribution. In the coming years, artificial intelligence will further erode their competitive advantages in online distribution, such as momentum pricing and economies of scale in distribution. Innovation in artificial intelligence renders global hospitality chains vulnerable to new competition, especially in leisure travel, new platforms are emerging around the globe.

"The reason why it is so difficult for existing firms to capitalize on disruptive innovations is that their processes and their business model that make them good at the existing business actually make them bad at competing for the disruption."

Clayton M. Christensen

3

BEATING THE TALENT DISRUPTION

● **Introduction: LA Hotel Workers Mount the Largest Hotel Strike Ever**

On July 4th 2023, thousands of employees at the most iconic hotels in Los Angeles celebrated America's birthday by joining the largest ever strike in the history of U.S. hospitality. While the dispute revolves around wages and work rules, the conspicuous issue is widening income inequality plaguing the industry. Unless a new mindset is adopted by management teams of hospitality chains, this lingering dispute may signal the end of the post-pandemic travel boom, contributing to a recession and substantial job losses across the country.

During the pandemic, hotels received $15 billion in federal bailouts and returned to profitability swiftly by cutting jobs and guest services. Fast forward to 2023, hotel profits in LA County have surpassed pre-pandemic levels and the city is collecting $225 million in transient occupancy taxes. Meanwhile, frontline workers, mostly women and minorities, struggle to afford a place to live in cities where they work and earn lower wages than UBER drivers.

● What's at Stake: The Magnitude of the Issue

65 full-service hotels, worth more than $5 billion and generating an estimated $500 million in operating profits combined, are at the heart of this conflict. The workers, including room attendants, cooks, dishwashers are demanding a 40% raise through an immediate $5 an hour increase with an additional $3 an hour in 2024 and 2025 plus 28% more benefits. The hotel coalition (which represents at least 42 of the hotels) offered a 30% raise with $2.50 an hour immediately and $6.25 over the next four years. A raise of $10 an hour equates to $1mm in additional labor costs or a decrease of 8-10% of net operating profits for these full-service hotels. This increase in fixed costs will reduce real estate values by an average of $15 million per hotel and render entire departments such as restaurants highly unprofitable with union labor costs as high as 80% of revenue. The outcome will be either layoffs and restaurant closures or leases to third parties willing to be subject to union work rules. Owners are rightly concerned about the significant impact on unit economics in the context of higher interest rates and minimal flexibility for refinancing.

● Inequality and its Discontents: The Post-Pandemic Labor Problem

The underlying issue goes beyond this hotel strike and is spreading across the country. It is a symptom of the growing income inequality within a highly profitable industry that has a Gini coefficient of 0.73, worse than South Africa (the country with the worst inequality according to the World Bank). The sector is grappling with a shrinking talent pool, losing 20% of its labor market share to the gig economy and other industries. Workers have lost their dignity and cite concerns such as increased workloads, affordable housing, and long commute times. The consequences are flowing through the service profit chain: customer satisfaction scores are at record lows and price increases have outpaced inflation by three times since 2021.

● Putting Things in Perspective:
A Framework for Talent Disruption

Harvard Business School Professor Christensen's research on innovation focused on technologies that address unmet customer needs through either low cost or new market disruptions. But there is another type of disruption that may radically alter performance in any industry: talent disruption. **Talent disruption** is the process by which traditional labor ends and talent shifts from legacy full-time employment to higher paying, more flexible work, facilitated by innovative technologies that empower individuals to build a personal brand. As disruption grows, talent ruthlessly migrates to the highest paying and most flexible sources of work and entrepreneurship, leapfrogging inefficiencies in hierarchies of legacy industries.

In our journey to develop an AI-driven talent marketplace for hospitality, our team developed a theory that predicts when talent disruption occurs and what incumbents can do to either mitigate or accelerate each type of disruption. The Talent Disruption framework has two dimensions: *talent creation*, or the ability of an organization to capture or lose share of elite talent and *unit labor economics*, or the total direct and indirect costs of talent divided by the unit of product or service. The slope of the disruption curve reflects the rate at which a sector progresses on both dimensions simultaneously. Those industries or organizations alongside or to the right of the curve address unmet customer needs through an operating model that creates a talent disruption resulting in a long-term shift in the labor markets.

On the x-axis, one can measure an organization's net talent creation in a geographic hub. This is a measure of its employer brand equity that reflects its share of the industry's talent pool, less turnover and attrition. KPIs measure whether organizations, and specifically, which functions and departments are gaining market share of elite talent (top 10% versus competitors). Second, talent creation measures the velocity of upwards mobility for these diverse elite talents as they rise the front line to managerial positions such as hotel GM, chief nurse, or store manager.

At the low end of the talent creation continuum, rigid talent management practices are used to recruit full time permanent employees that have strict job definitions, multiple reporting layers, an established hierarchy or pecking order supported by many standardized processes. At the extreme, they are unionized, with job-based pay scales and tenure-based criteria for advancement.

Conversely, at the high end of the talent creation continuum, there are team-based organizations where the workforce performs multiple, flexible jobs and a network of vetted part time or gig workers may even be key contributors. These organizations possess "bench strength," with deep talent pipelines, that can withstand changes in demand by orchestrating faster or slower career mobility for its employees. The scope of employees' duties may vary radically by project, and they work in organizations that are flat, with minimal bureaucracy and documented rules of engagement.

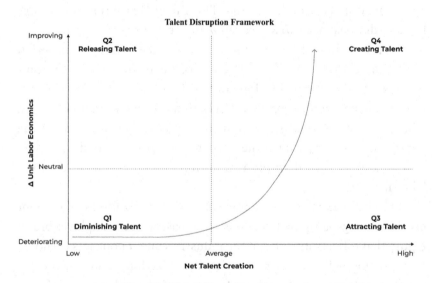

Figure 3.1: Talent Disruption Framework

The Y-axis measures change in unit labor economics, or the change in total compensation divided by a single unit or production or customers served. For example, in hospitals unit labor economics can be calculated by dividing total compensation for full time equivalents (including contracted labor such as Nurses and technicians) by the number of patients discharged. In hotels or vacation rentals, occupied room nights and restaurant covers per seat are examples of the denominator used to measure unit economics. The extent to which an organization's unit labor economics improves or declines, for any reason (such as an economic correction, process, or technology innovations) is charted over time, with a steeper positive slope of the curve implying positive gains.

The change in unit labor economics can also reflect different degrees of automation, starting with operational processes such as back-office and support functions, all the way to core customer-facing activities. Examples include U.S. hospitals that experienced a 180 percent increase in costs per unit of service from 2019 to 2022 primarily due to a 258 percent increase in contract labor for nurses, technicians, and other roles over this three-year period. Consequently, their unit labor economics are deteriorating, and they lack the processes and technology tools to grow the talent pool other than through traditional methods which occur in low frequency.

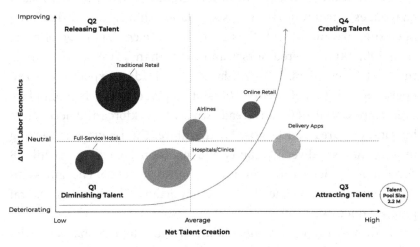

Figure 3.2: Talent Disruption Framework

● Talent Disruption in the Service Industry

The immediate pre and post Covid-19 pandemic period, from 2019 to 2023 provides a window into the performance of service industries, especially hospitality, retail, and healthcare. We used AI and machine learning to analyze and chart the human capital performance of over 1000 internally managed properties at over 100 publicly traded companies in the hotel, hospital, retail, and delivery sectors.

We classified industries and organizations into one of four buckets to chart their historical performance and determine whether they are either facing a talent disruption or likely to confront one soon. It's also useful to chart the relative progress or decline of an organization's operational processes over time, including whether they are sustaining their model by relocating production to arbitrage differential currency, labor cost and regulatory gains in a global supply chain.

● Accelerating and Combating the Talent Disruption in Service Industries 2019-2023

A case in point is that the healthcare industry is facing significant challenges, including rising costs, a labor shortage, and declining operating margins. The U.S. is projected to face a shortage of more than 200,000 registered nurses and more than 50,000 physicians in the next three years. In 2023, healthcare leaders expect a drop in operating margins of between 25 and 75 percent, which could place even more workload for an already stressed workforce and necessitate hospital closures and layoffs. Furthermore, the industry is seeking improvements in diversity, equity, and inclusion. For example, while 28 percent of physicians are immigrants, only 6 percent of Hispanics and 5 percent of Black people identify as physicians; 75 percent of general practice doctors are men.

However, innovative models are being adopted that shift the industry from hospital-based care to lower acuity sites and home-based care, enabled by innovative technologies. $1 trillion of productivity improvements are being ushered in by telehealth, virtual testing, and remote patient monitoring. Furthermore, the industry is responding to improve transparency and data sharing, including price transparency and data interoperability. The integration of price and quality-rating information across healthcare providers will help consumers make better decisions about where to go for care. Furthermore, the regional expansion of academic medical centers through mergers and acquisitions into distribution networks such as UCLA Health, including doctors' offices and clinics are resulting in burgeoning talent pools for nurses, technicians, and residents. R&D has grown to over $200 billion, or 6 percent of revenue, including over $20 billion invested in building AI-driven "hospitals of the future," and the industry has attracted over $50 billion of capital since 2021 focused on creating workflow efficiencies and using data for clinical decision support.

Therefore, as healthcare becomes less expensive and automated, less invasive, and more precise and customers have access to their data, unit labor costs for hospitals and most healthcare providers will decline sharply. This will result in reductions in admission costs per patient. Public-private partnerships in healthcare are investing in technologies such as remote monitored robotic surgeries that are also changing the nature of work. Further investments in for-profit hospitals from private equity will create more cost efficiencies that mitigate the labor shortage.

The retail industry, which is expected to close 50,000 stores in 2022 alone and continue investing in e-commerce automation. Given the restructuring of commercial real estate across the country, retail may permanently shrink as an employer. However, new roles in fulfillment, logistics and AI are being created, and retailers will increasingly compete for talent with traditional manufacturing, logistics, and technology businesses.

In contrast, absent significant innovation, labor productivity in U.S. hotels will continue to diminish. Even taking into consideration an economic recession, changes in U.S. immigration policies and departures from legacy brand standards resulting in reduced service levels and further investment in employer branding, the industry will have 2.4 million job openings annually. Hotels will continue suffering from "diminishing talent," losing market share of future GMs to other industries and experience growing labor costs buttressed by the expansionist agenda of organized labor, and the intensifying talent shift to the gig economy.

● The Root Causes of the Hotel Industry's Talent Disruption

Despite a labor shortage of 1.6 million workers (and a demand for 2.4 million workers annually including turnover), the main hurdle in the hotel industry is the lack of leadership. Various parties extract billions of dollars in fees from hotels for branding, asset and hotel management, taxes, and union dues yet accountability is murky. The industry's governance structure is becoming unmanageable, with brands, owners, third-party operators, cities, and municipalities pointing fingers at each other. Hotel chains focused on franchising avoid accountability while enjoying the benefits of revenues from the topline and owner funded marketing budgets. Meanwhile, cities and municipalities extract $46 billion in taxes but prioritize advertising over labor related investments.

Unions are growing and workers have few alternatives but to join them to have a voice. Unlike airlines, frontline employees have no ownership stake in hotel properties. Hotel owners, driven by short-term profit goals, perpetuate turnover by hiring third-party managers to cut costs and exiting properties an average of every 5.5 years. Hotel operators have also been inefficient in recruiting talent, relying on legacy technologies that filter out millions of semi-qualified hidden workers. It's imperative that industry CEOs advance alternative, market-based solutions, such as pay for performance, that demonstrate a renewed sense of purpose in building human capital.

● Strategic Choices for Hotel CEOs and Boards of Directors

There are three, non-exclusive strategic alternatives for the industry that change the game and revitalize the industry.

1. **Accelerate Automation through AI**: Hotels could reduce labor costs through automation and robotics, eliminating many front-line positions and eventually entire departments such as the front office or housekeeping. They can also further reduce brand standards, service levels, and amenities. Such experiments are taking place in China and other East Asian markets, and feedback from tech savvy customers has been overall positive. However, this approach risks a confrontation with unions, work stoppages, cannibalizing brands and prolonging the recovery of individual and group business travel in the context of a potential recession. Given the potential job losses, it will also invite government intervention which could lead to unintended consequences, at the local and state levels.

2. **Empower Employees through Ownership**: The industry could adopt AI-driven HR technologies and build transparent talent marketplaces that reward high performers and facilitate meritocracy. AI can be used to establish market-based approaches such as profit sharing, ownership and other variable pay including bonuses and tips. In addition, hotel owners should make front-line employee's partial owners, teaching them financial literacy and giving them a voice in property level governance. As employee ownership generates new wealth and expands hospitality's middle class, it will help spawn a new generation of future hotel owners, including those being targeted in DEI related initiatives. This approach requires partnering with technology start-ups and additional legal and data related costs but could drive productivity, drive fixed costs down and attract talent into the industry.

3. **Reinvent the Franchising Model**: Hotels should adjust the use of proceeds in their franchising fee model and partner with cities to redirect funds, such as program fees and tax revenues, to support workforce-related initiatives including housing allowances tied to employee retention. Asset managers could reallocate capital reserves (2-4%) of revenues to performance-based bonuses, and housing allowances for hourly workers. Although this shift in resource allocation from marketing to human capital is not what unions are seeking, it represents a market-based approach toward addressing the industry's talent disruption.

● Conclusion: Hospitality's Moment of Truth Has Arrived

Ironically, as the hotel strikes in Los Angeles continue year end 2023, emboldened labor groups are increasing the likelihood of automation that will permanently shrink employment in hospitality, an industry which has a rich history of self-made entrepreneurship that includes people of all backgrounds and social classes. Inspired by an M.I.T. backed venture called Spyce that developed a fully automated robotic kitchen to reduce the price of a meal by 40 percent, with the support of celebrity chef Daniel Boulud, high growth restaurant chains such as Sweetgreens and Chipotle have committed to automating their kitchens, leaving only food preparation and purchasing to their culinary teams. It's time for stakeholders to step up with innovative solutions that prioritize worker well-being, address income inequality, and elongate the travel boom. By investing in artificial intelligence and adapting the franchising business model, CEOs in the hotel industry can create new wealth alongside a more equitable and prosperous future for all stakeholders.

"The development of full artificial intelligence could spell the end of the human race...It would take off on its own, and re-design itself at an ever increasing rate. Humans, who are limited by slow biological evolution, couldn't compete, and would be superseded."

Stephen Hawking

4

ENVISAGING THE AI
HOTEL OF THE FUTURE

magine that you are eagerly organizing a weekend getaway for your daughter's 16th birthday. You're on the hunt for a boutique luxury resort, ideally located within a two-hour drive from your home, to accommodate her and her 100 closest friends for an unforgettable celebration. Given her immense love for Bollywood, you're seeking a venue that can truly make her feel like a celebrity on her special day. Your checklist includes booking 50 double-bed rooms, 5000 square feet event space capable of hosting a dinner for 100 guests with live entertainment, and a facility that can sustain a vibrant dance party well into the night.

● AI Travel Planning

Opting for the efficiency of technology, you turn to the AI assistant on your preferred internet search engine. Your initial input includes the date, geographical location, desired resort class and amenities, specific room types and floors, catering needs for food and beverages, and spa treatments. The AI system efficiently processes your criteria, returning a curated list of boutique lifestyle and luxury resort options that meet your specifications. Among these, you focus on the one boasting the highest accolades for hosting social events.

Carefully reviewing the presented choices, you compare amenities, ratings, and pricing for each element of the potential experience. Your attention is drawn to a particular luxury resort located on Ocean Drive in Santa Monica. This venue stands out with its celebrity chef-led restaurant renowned for catering upscale events, a rooftop nightclub offering panoramic views of the Santa Monica Pier and the Pacific Ocean, capable of accommodating a 100-person group. It's highly praised for social events and includes a star meeting planner, aligning impressively with 92% of your search preferences, including valet parking.

You land on the property's website, and its AI-enabled booking engine asks you questions about your daughter's personality and interests, such as her preferred genres of music, food and favorite treatments and services in the spa and salon. It turns out your daughter is a big fan of Bollywood Bhangra dance and movies, she loves Southern Indian vegetarian cuisine, and she is passionate about curated fashion such as jewel embroidered Sarees and Lengha dress. Based on your answers, the hotel site generates an itinerary which includes a package with preference-matching percentages, pictures and videos of each activity, customer reviews and a la carte pricing options.

The booking engine lets you delve into an Augmented Reality (AR) experience to explore and personalize every aspect of your event. Picture yourself virtually walking through the finest suites and rooms, getting a feel for the event space, and browsing the dining options. You also get to customize your event down to the last detail – from selecting the theme-matching decor, lighting, and music, to arranging how the food is presented and where guests will sit. You even have the freedom to tweak things like the color scheme, the layout of the tables, lighting of the event, and the seating arrangements. And for an extra touch of excitement, you add a special Bollywood Bhangra dance performance and a live chef food presentation.

Once you're happy with the preview, you reach out to the event planning team to finalize everything. This includes confirming the hotel room allocation, pinpointing the exact room locations, and setting times for the dinner and party. The event planner promptly sends over a quote. You then secure your booking with a deposit and complete the payment. Excitedly, you share the party preview with your daughter and the guests, stirring up anticipation for the celebration. Remarkably, the entire process of searching, planning, booking, and communicating is streamlined and efficient, taking just 30 minutes.

● Arrival Experience

Arriving at the hotel a day before the party, your family of three looks forward to a relaxing day and a chance to check out the event space for any last tweaks. In the lobby, the arrival manager, and a hotel intern, accompanied by a humanoid robot named Natasha clad in traditional Indian attire, warmly welcome you, celebrating your daughter's 16th birthday. The intern hands you the hotel's signature welcome drink. After some friendly exchanges, Natasha scans your retina, enabling a unique check-in process via a text message code. Once scanned, she efficiently checks you in and instructs her robotic colleague, Henry, donned in a virtual hotel uniform, to take care of your luggage and guide you to your room.

As Henry escorts you to your room, Natasha briefs your wife on the latest preparations for your daughter's birthday celebration. She connects you to the VIP event host, who greets you via a tablet. The host enthusiastically shares that her team, along with the chef, are dedicated to crafting an unforgettable experience for your daughter and the guests. Natasha also reminds you to utilize the hotel's mobile app for event planning. Through the app, you can stay updated with live progress on the event's organization and make any necessary changes on the go.

● Luxury Suite Experience

Upon being verified by the robot via biometric check-in, you use the barcode sent to your phone to access your two-bedroom suite. You're immediately welcomed by a digital display of Bollywood art, a favorite of your daughter's, adorning the walls and her preferred Indian pop tunes playing softly. In the living room, a high-tech mirror catches your eye, showcasing a range of clothing options through augmented reality, from contemporary designs to traditional Indian wear, all available for rent from an online retailer with the promise of delivery to your suite within three hours.

In the master bedroom, you're comforted to find a bed equipped with pillows designed to support your pregnant wife's needs. Nearby, the "NASA Analyzer" stands out - a cutting-edge, non-invasive medical diagnostic tool, compact enough for deep-space missions, capable of analyzing various sample types and measuring a wide array of analytes. Intrigued, you scan its QR code to learn more about this advanced technology.

Your exploration leads you to the second bedroom, where birthday decorations, balloons, and a personalized note from the General Manager await, all celebrating your daughter's special day. Feeling a bit peckish, you peruse the kitchen, finding it stocked with your family's favorite drinks and a digital menu that offers room service from the hotel's casual eatery, alongside recommendations from local venues and the hotel's own restaurants, all tailored to fit your family's unique dietary preferences based on your "live to 120" AI genomic profile.

You switch on the TV, greeted by a personalized welcome message. Eager to catch up on your favorite Netflix series right where you left off at home, you navigate to your customized entertainment channel. This unique feature seamlessly integrates with your personal Netflix, Hulu, Paramount, and other streaming accounts, allowing you to continue your viewing experience without missing a beat, enveloped in the comfort of your suite.

● AI Enhanced Event Experience

The following day, with excitement building for the birthday celebration, you quickly open the mobile app to confirm that the party preparations are on track, and everything is set for the event. After ensuring all is in order, you head down to the lobby. Greeted by a robot, you receive warm birthday wishes for your daughter. The robot then guides you to the rooftop, where an eagerly awaited party is set to unfold.

As you ascend to the rooftop, the VIP event manager welcomes you with a delightful glass of Mango Lassi. Holding the refreshing drink, you stroll around to survey the setup. The rooftop has been transformed with a vibrant Bollywood theme, complete with event organizers dressed in Punjabi attire, and the energizing rhythms of Bollywood music inviting you to dance.

While mingling with other parents on the rooftop, another alert captures your attention. A guest messages to say they'll be bringing an additional five people. This news briefly unsettles you, as the party was meticulously planned for 100 attendees. Without hesitation, you access the hotel app to communicate with your VIP event host. You request extra seating to accommodate the unforeseen guests. They respond promptly, assuring you of a swift resolution. Comforted by their quick action, you let go of your concerns and once again immerse yourself in the joy of the party.

● Food and Beverage Experience

At the party, you and your guests relish the array of foods and drinks thoughtfully customized by the AI hotel to align with the theme and preferences of your gathering. The menu, prepared with attention to dietary needs, offers vegetarian, dairy-free, and gluten-free options. Organically sourced from local farms, the food is presented in a visually appealing manner, segregated into vegan, vegetarian, and meat selections. The spread includes vibrant and tasty dishes like Samosas,

Panipuri, and a variety of Biryani, catering to the refined tastes of culinary enthusiasts. The beverage options, including Mango Lassi, Masala Chai, Nimbu Pani, and Thandai, are equally refreshing and delightful.

The chef and sous-chef add an entertaining twist to the evening by personally presenting the entrees. They engage the guests with stories about the origins and cultural significance of each dish and drink, interspersed with humor and interactive food chemistry tips for the kids, such as balancing spices with yogurt. The culinary team's appearance culminates in a well-deserved standing ovation, photo sessions with the teens and their parents, and heartfelt thanks from the attendees.

The party is full of excitement, with you thoroughly enjoying the chef's presentation and the delectable food. You express your gratitude and admiration for her team's efforts. The arrival of a group of Bollywood dancers, performing your daughter's favorite Bhangra dance, elevates the celebration. The party peaks as the chef presents a triple-layered birthday cake while everyone sings 'Happy Birthday' to your daughter, accompanied by the legendary voice of Lata Mangeshkar in the background. The event concludes on a high note, leaving everyone content and delighted.

● Post Event Experience

The next day, you receive the captured videos and photos through the event planner app, allowing you to instantly download and share these cherished moments on social media. Shortly thereafter, you're invited to review and tip the hotel team, including the event planner, chef, and even the robots, for their exceptional service and contribution to a memorable celebration.

● How AI Powers the Hotel of the Future

Thanks to advances in artificial intelligence and robotics, this customer innovation scenario is not farfetched. Academic research on how robot-Brand fit the influence of brand personality on consumer reactions to robot adoption from experts at the University of Kong and Sejong University in Seoul has validated that high-contact robots (that handle tasks such as check-in and dining service) are best suited for exciting brands that are trendy, youthful, and imaginative.

● Operational Core

The AI hotel of the future will be a place where human and machine intelligence work together to create a seamless and personalized experience for guests, supported by an AI-adjacent workforce. In this context, AI can enable hotels to run more efficiently by using an AI-enabled operating system that integrates disparate systems and external data sources. The operating system will act as a motherboard that connects various components, such as property management systems (PMS), revenue management systems (RMS), customer relationship management (CRM), point of sale systems (POS), and human resources information systems (HRIS) to interact with each other while streamlining processes through algorithmic predictions that determine everything from average daily pricing and real-time marketing offers to optimal staffing and product supply levels.

The motherboard will leverage both types of data: soft and hard. Soft data comes from digital sources, such as booking systems, guest profiles and preferences, market trends, and customer reviews. Hard data captures the tacit knowledge and expertise of hotel employees and hospitality experts, such as housekeepers, restaurant managers, chefs, and service representatives. Hard data is obtained from employee's real-time interactions with guests, their responses to operational challenges, as well as customer feedback. The AI operating system will then engage data scientists, AI, and robotic engineers to synthesize data, collaborate with hotel employees, and curate guest service. AI-powered simulations extend across the supply chain, including procurement for laundry, hotel cleaning supplies, and food and beverages, enabling hotels to predict demand, edit selections and route deliveries in hours instead of days.

● Talent Engine

AI hotels are powered by a Talent Engine at their core, which acts as a vibrant community, attracting hidden workers, legal immigrants, and freelancers, including a hybrid and remote workforce. It uses data from independent third-party sources and algorithms to help organizations identify rising and elite talents within and outside their organization. Data Science and Operations are the core of the Talent Engine, where data is used to find, evaluate, and rank the best talents based on their merits. The Talent Engine also features a two-sided talent marketplace that connects the top talents with projects, including opportunities outside the organization. Moreover, the Talent Engine offers learning and development opportunities for talents, using AR/VR and experiential learning, to advance their career goals. The Talent Engine has a profile for each Humanoid robot, which shows the talents who have contributed to training the robot's large language models and intelligence. The profile also displays the data and knowledge the robot has learned, along with the time and date of the training sessions. The talents who participate in training the robots receive lifetime royalties, which allows them to create lasting wealth as frontline employees.

● Reservation System

The progression towards a data-driven, algorithmic approach in yield management not only maximizes revenue and reduces the need for intermediaries such as channel managers, online travel agencies, and meta search engines. But an AI-driven booking engine doesn't just sell and book a room. It constructs an experience that matches customers with accommodations and experiences which starts with their stay preferences, such as bedding type, music genre, soap and shampoo brands, towel types, shower temperature, water pressure, and other preferences. The reservation system also matches customers to branded robots, otherwise known as hosts, that can adopt the service style and tone of voice, methods, and frequency of communication the guest seeks on the specific travel occasion.

● Personalizing the Future of Travel Marketing

AI-driven hotels transform the landscape of hospitality by learning and predicting guest preferences, creating a marketing approach that feels almost telepathic. When a potential guest interacts online, the AI begins crafting a unique experience. A couple planning their anniversary weekend at a luxury resort could virtually stroll through a romantic sunset beach walk, construct their meal, design their dinner food presentation, and select an eco-tourism tour before booking their stay.

Moreover, AI integration extends to real-time, on-site customization during the stay. Here are some ways AI hotels can create bespoke customer experiences, typically reserved for luxury customers:

- **Hyper-segmentation**: AI hotels can use advanced analytics and machine learning to hyper-segment their customers into psychographic dimensions that speak to their service style, such as bohemian luxe, which describes rising technology and entertainment entrepreneurs who prefer to cherish curated local discoveries and informal and relaxed service style typically seen in independent and boutique hotels.
- **Lifestyle Programming**: Each individual hotel could have an open-source content channel that features appraised local

musicians, entertainers, and other creatives. Using data from various sources, such as social media and purchasing trends on applications such as Spotify and Netflix, hoteliers could introduce content from up-and-coming local artists that match a customer's interests.

● Advancing Sustainability

The AI hotel of the future is driven by the vision of providing guests with the information and tools they need to advance sustainability in all aspects of their experience. Using sensors, Internet of Thing (IoT), and advanced analytics, the customers can accomplish the following objectives:

- **Minimizing Food Waste**: AI analyzes the guests' preferences and dietary needs and predicts the optimal amount and variety of food to prepare, thus avoiding food waste. AI is fully integrated into the chef's procurement system and suggests locally sourced ingredients that have lower environmental impact and support local farmers, proposes catering menus that are more plant-based, seasonal, and organic, and tracks the environmental impact of each ingredient, such as the CO_2 emissions, water usage, land use, and biodiversity loss. Excess food is automatically routed to local food banks and charities in an integrated supply chain.
- **Reducing Carbon Footprint**: The AI hotel model motivates guests to reduce their carbon footprint during their stay by tracking and analyzing data such as transportation modes, travel distances, energy and water consumption and creating a carbon footprint report at the end of the stay. Guests will be incentivized with discounts for lowering their carbon footprint during their stay and consuming less energy.
- **Decreasing Energy Consumption**: The AI hotel model saves energy by using intelligent devices and sensors that control

the lighting, heating, cooling, and ventilation of the rooms and facilities according to the occupancy, weather, and time of the day. The AI hotel model also relies on renewable energy sources, such as solar panels, wind turbines, and geothermal systems, to run the hotel and lower its reliance on fossil fuels.

● Enabling Health and Wellbeing

Frequent long-haul travel negatively impacts health and reduces life spans due to changes in time zones, nutrition, sleeping pattern, air quality, and other factors. The AI hotel of the future could integrate into well-being data apps connected to the room's remote diagnostics and share information to selected health care providers. The science of sleep is also fertile ground for innovation: smart beds with sleep tracking sensors, temperature control, and an adjustable base can enhance sleep quality for guests. Smart bathrooms could provide urine and nutrition analysis to detect any health issues or deficiencies and recommendations to a customer and their health care provider. Smart mirrors can project the overall health statistics of the guests, such as blood pressure, heart rate, body mass index, and stress level, offering suggestions for better decision-making and well-being. Smart food menus can generate curated food options based on the guests' nutrition needs, preferences, and allergies. In a world where healthcare is becoming more remote and personalized, these technologies will enable customers to improve their well-being through actionable data that leads to better decision-making, saves time and money and prevents disease.

● AI Hotels: Incubators for Strategic Innovation

Employees are still the most critical component of the AI hotel of the future. Without the expertise and creativity of hotel employees who are part-owners of the property and compensated for their creation of intellectual property, building the AI hotel of the future will be impossible. Humanoid robot branding, which has captured the world's attention, is the next frontier in lifestyle hospitality. As hotel managers evolve from static programming of their properties to content creators in a world of AI-powered entertainment, new revenue models are created including streaming events and partnering with studios to produce pulse-racing, spine-tingling material to communities that relish drama. In the process, the stars of the show such as celebrity chefs, event planners, and their teams can receive a share of the royalties.

The AI hotel of the future must foster a culture of innovation among its employees. The hotel will not require a dedicated R&D department, but artificial intelligence will facilitate collaboration between hospitality experts, data scientists and engineers by prompting them to explore new ways of enhancing hospitality and improving service innovation. AI will automate experimentation with innovative ideas, learn from failures, and share best practices across a network of properties.

• Responsible AI

These innovations undoubtedly enhance the overall guest experience; however, they also bring forth significant ethical and security considerations. The OECD defines AI as "a machine-based system that can, for a given set of human defined-objectives, make predictions, recommendations or decisions influencing real or virtual environments." It classifies AI cases into one of the following 7 types: hyper-personalization, recognition, conversation and human interaction, predictive decision and analytics, goal-driven systems, autonomous systems, and patterns and anomalies. Responsible AI requires establishing global auditing standards and requirements, starting with authenticating AI-generated content, user testing and content traceability in areas that protect consumers and employees.

It's imperative that the hotel of the future addresses the following dimensions of Responsible AI effectively:

- **Privacy and Security:** The gathering and storage of guest data for personalization and automation can give rise to substantial privacy concerns. Guests may fret about the utilization of their data, who possesses access to it, and whether it receives adequate protection against potential breaches. The advent of generative AI has made social engineering increasingly accessible, rendering humans more susceptible to breaches than AI-powered systems. AI-powered hotels of the future have embedded comprehensive security features. Guests can activate a fully-encrypted stay feature, ensuring that their data and information are thoroughly concealed and stored separately, thereby guaranteeing protection against privacy and personal data breaches even in the event of a security breach.

- **Bias and discrimination:** AI algorithms can inadvertently reflect the inherent biases of the data they are trained on. To mitigate bias and discrimination in AI-powered hotels of the future, a comprehensive approach involves diverse and representative training data, regular bias audits, and transparency in AI decision-making. Implementing ethical AI guidelines, offering human oversight, and continuously monitoring algorithms for emerging biases are crucial. Providing mechanisms for guest feedback, considering third-party audits, and collaborating with legal and ethical experts further ensure compliance with laws and regulations. These measures collectively aim to reduce legal and reputational risks while promoting fairness and equity in the guest experience

- **Job displacement:** The automation of tasks through AI has raised concerns about potential job displacement among hotel staff. The scope of Responsible AI should include auditing all recruitment-related software starting with applicant tracking systems and job sites for systematic bias. The truth is that the process was deeply flawed prior to the advent of AI, filtering out semi qualified workers, most notably women, minorities and military veterans and exacerbating historic labor shortages. However, AI Hotels of the future aims to empower employees by enabling them to acquire new skills, including AI-related knowledge. The goal is to build an AI-adjacent workforce, certified by the Responsible AI Institute (RAII). Employees focus on enhancing AI systems, collaborating with data scientists and robotic engineers, and elevating the overall guest experience through valuable feedback. This shift towards a future where laborious tasks are handled by robots presents an opportunity for a more fulfilling and innovative work environment.

- **Accessibility:** Ensuring that AI-driven technologies are accessible to all guests, including those with disabilities, can be challenging. To achieve this, AI systems are meticulously crafted with inclusivity as a fundamental principle which includes features like voice commands and user-friendly interfaces, AI-powered apps with real-time voice instructions for navigating the property for visually impaired guests. By placing inclusivity at the forefront of their design philosophy, AI hotels of the future aim to provide an equitable and enjoyable experience for all guests, irrespective of their physical or cognitive capabilities.

- **Data Ownership and Control:** Travelers need to know when AI is used and how it's employed, as well as how and where to provide timely feedback and complaints. To ensure transparency and prevent potential disputes, AI hotels establish explicit guidelines regarding data ownership, leaving no room for ambiguity. Furthermore, AI hotels prioritize granting guests significant control over their data, allowing individuals to manage and dictate how their information is used. This commitment to guest empowerment underscores the hotel's dedication to responsible data management and privacy, fostering trust and confidence among all patrons.

- **Advancement of Secure AI:** Prioritizing the development of AI models that pose no harm, which includes the publication of a Model Card for every new iteration of an AI model upon deployment. This Model Card comprehensively outlines the model's usage and provides insights into the safety assessments conducted to evaluate its reliability and security.

The AI hotels of the future ensures compliance with national and international responsible AI guidelines which includes actions such as, sharing safety test results and other critical information with the government to ensure it passes the standard test scenarios, developing standard tools and tests to ensure that every innovation is tested for safety and trustworthiness prior to making it public, and develop principle and best practices to mitigate the harms and maximize the benefits of AI for workers.

● Conclusion: Back to The Future

In *Back to the Future*, Marty (Michael J. Fox) says "This is heavy" a bunch of times throughout the trilogy. Whenever he's bewildered or confused in time travel gone awry, he uses his catchphrase. At one point, Doc (Christopher Lloyd) asks him about the turn of phrase: "There's that word again, 'heavy.' Why are things so heavy in the future? Is there a problem with the Earth's gravitational pull?"

As quantum computing progresses, industries are converging. Like most disruptive technologies, AI hotels will benefit from learning and collaboration with industries at the forefront of robotics and automation such as the hospitals of the future. As a case in point, advanced computer vision, including the processing abilities of its visual and voice sensors - the robots' nerves and sensory organs - are rapidly advancing with machine learning. More power-dense batteries have made it possible for a humanoid robot to move its legs quickly enough to balance dynamically and navigate stairs, ramps, and unsteady ground. These trends don't necessarily mean there will be fewer people employed in hospitality. On the contrary, thousands of talents can train Large Language Models and develop humanoids with different service styles and personalities. As artificial intelligence continues to progress at a breathtaking pace, the line between science fiction and reality becomes increasingly blurred. The dawn of AI-driven hospitality is going to reshape travel in ways we could not imagine a few years ago.

"The biggest barriers to strategic renewal are almost always top management's unexamined beliefs."

Gary Hamel

5

OVERTURNING
ORTHODOXIES TO
ACCELERATE DIVERSITY

As a double immigrant raised in Toronto, having spent a decade in New York and eventually starting a lifestyle hotel brand in Shanghai, I enjoyed the benefit of living in and working among the most diverse and multicultural places on earth. I have also worked for diversity award winning corporations such as Deloitte, Accenture and Hilton to name a few.

Research confirms that discrimination is best understood not by classroom lectures or corporate training, but by those who have experienced it firsthand. In 2007, when I was senior vice president of corporate development at Hilton, I was presenting to the board of directors at a Waldorf Astoria resort in Phoenix, Arizona. After a very thorough question-and-answer period that followed my presentation, I undid my tie and walked to the valet to retrieve my car rental. The valet crew was out retrieving vehicles so I waited politely alongside a few other hotel guests at this iconic resort.

In a span of a few minutes, not one but three white men handed me the car keys to their vintage sports cars, mistaking me for the valet. I passed the keys over to the actual valet who quipped, "This is one of the few places where they trust brown people." It turns out all three were CEOs of real estate and finance companies and were frequent guests at the resort.

While the implicit bias of this experience was demoralizing, it pales in comparison to the explicit barriers that women and ethnic minorities face in reaching the senior ranks of the hospitality industry.

Given the lack of diversity at the top of hotel companies, it is even more important for executives to get off the beaten path. When I became CEO of Cachet Hotels in Shanghai in 2012, I championed increasing diversity and made it one of my top three objectives as CEO.

In many Asian markets, hotel owners strongly associate prestigious international hotel brands with the tall handsome European men who usually manage them. Despite this association, in 2012, Cachet Hotels set a bold goal of 50% female and minority general managers at our hotels and restaurants. At the time women comprised 70% of the hotel workforce in China, but only 5% of full-service hotel general managers.

Cachet Hotels' diversity initiative grew from a top-down purpose that I articulated at our first Chinese press conference in Shanghai to being a widely adopted practice that was embraced by hotel operators whose entire work experience was working for European men in mainland China. Five years later, we met our objective across our entire portfolio of hotels and restaurants in China, the rest of Asia and the Americas. We were also pleased that a few years later, in 2015, Accor announced a goal of 35% women hotel general managers in the Asia Pacific region.

I returned to the States a few years ago and partnered with hotel industry veterans, data scientists and technologists to build MogulRecruiter, an elite talent marketplace whose mission is to perfect meritocracy and accelerate diversity. According to our research at MogulRecruiter, women and minorities comprise 60% and 40% of the U.S. hotel front-line. However, only 20% of U.S. hotel general managers are women and 10% minorities. Blacks represent 15% of the frontline and only 1% of hotel general managers.

It took us a few years to analyze the data but we have developed algorithms to rank diverse pools of talent and predict their worth and annual compensation. Today, our talent database has over 500,000 elite hospitality leaders in supervisor roles and above featuring over 50% women and 33% who identify as minorities. However, our work is just getting started.

Through these leadership experiences and "swimming in the data," I learned a thing or two about sourcing and developing diverse talent in the hospitality industry. Today, the hotel industry's consolidation has made the executive ranks a small world. Many of my former corporate colleagues, owners and business partners are now CEOs of major hotel brands and real estate groups. Most are quite sophisticated, care deeply about building winning cultures and have established clear metrics that define winning in real estate, property operations and online distribution. But prior to 2020, few have set diversity as one of their top management priorities. Many have remained silent despite their good intentions and continue to invest large sums of money marketing their brands as champions of diversity on social media platforms.

The hotel industry remains extremely conservative with few outsider CEOs. Being in the same industry and company for a long period of time can ingrain even the most exceptional business leaders with orthodoxies or deeply held beliefs about "how we do business in this industry." These widely adopted orthodoxies are perpetuated by the investment community, media, academics, industry associations and universities. Not all orthodoxies are toxic, but the ones that create massive blind spots which ultimately become driving lanes for disruption.

Hotel CEOs can start by identifying the toxic orthodoxies that must be challenged to accelerate diversity and then brainstorm what opportunities could be made possible if they are overturned. To start the process, the following are five industry orthodoxies regarding diversity in the hotel industry:

1. **"The focus of a CEO's diversity agenda should be the board and human resources leader, including a strong diversity department in the corporate office."**

To overturn this orthodoxy, start with the hotel properties.

Jim Reynolds, the African American chairman and CEO of Chicago-based Loop Capital, recently said in a CNBC interview: "I have not ever been able, and I'm trying, to find a correlation between Blacks on the board of directors and a company doing more for Blacks and African Americans. I haven't seen it."

Adding a few diverse members to your board of directors and building a diversity department in HR is important but it is table stakes – the cost of entry. Moreover, hotel companies have been doing this for decades with little if any meaningful progress.

For hotel CEOs, the leadership challenge is achieving diversity at the property managerial levels, where an array of owners, lenders, third-party management companies, unions and other stakeholders can intentionally or unintentionally block progress. To accelerate progress, CEOs must focus more time on implementing change in the properties starting with those they manage and with real estate owners and third-party operators who get it.

2. **"Diversity data on employees and the talent pipeline is best kept confidential both internally and externally."**

To overturn this orthodoxy, collect and share employee-volunteered data with all levels of the entire organization and franchised properties. Then make it public before the governments and regulators require us to do so.

The NAACP already publishes an annual report where it grades hotel operators and their franchisees on minority representation of skilled versus unskilled labor, property management and corporate ranks. In 2019, the NAACP declared that "little progress has been made since the organization's 2005 evaluation," and gave Hilton, Hyatt and Wyndham each a C and Marriott a B. For top management representation, the range of grades was from C (best score) to many Fs. How does this square with the same brands winning diversity awards from major publications?

The issue is data transparency. While I applaud the NAACP, their grades are based on EEOC data and surveys with grades based on results against their own targets. Meanwhile, hotel industry leaders have not been forthcoming in sharing data. This is the same approach they used to protect customer reviews while Tripadvisor and other online travel agencies established the high ground with consumers, adding travelers' photos and property ranking algorithms. To this day, Marriott is the only hotel brand that shows customer reviews on its own website.

Hotel CEOs manage a complex ecosystem of stakeholders and recognize that the first step in leading any change process is to collect and disseminate data widely. Data also helps stimulate debate and new ideas and may even create entire markets for innovation. It is also in the shareholders' best interest for hotel CEOs to take the lead rather than hide beyond legal excuses and wait for regulators and politicians to legislate requirements that may serve their parochial political interests.

Regular reports on diversity gaps should be as important as customer reviews. Diversity should be an integral part of a talent pipeline, integrated into dashboards and pushed all the way down to hotel management teams.

3. **"Our labor costs are already too high, and diversity will only increase our recruiting, training and legal costs."**

To overturn this orthodoxy, use zero-based budgeting and reset the entire recruiting and HR model to reduce expenses.

Labor-related costs are over 50% of the cost structure of full-service hotels and have been increasing at 5 to 10% per annum, outpacing revenues since 2000. However, do not forget that the U.S. hotel industry generates profit margins of 25 to 50% and just came off a decade-long streak with record profits of $70 to $80 billion annually. Unlike airlines such as Southwest and Delta and other lower-margin service industries, no publicly traded hotel management company has ever implemented an employee stock ownership plan. To my knowledge, no private equity firm has implemented a promotion structure that gives hotel executive teams compensation for increasing real estate value.

Still, contrary to conventional wisdom, accelerating diversity does not require spending more money or increasing a hotel's fixed cost structure. What it does require is cost innovation that results from restructuring the talent acquisition process. The outcome of a new process should be spending less money on the internal resources, vendors and search firms that are recycling the same candidates, sell data as their business model and increase employee turnover which remains at 40 to 75%.

We know that talent attracts talent. Diversity also attracts diversity. The marginal costs of building a diverse workforce should drop considerably if the diversity at managerial levels is addressed up front.

4. "The best way to reduce turnover and ensure fit is to use assessments and personality tests."

To overturn this orthodoxy, stop using assessments and personality tests.

Hotels should take a cue from colleges and universities and decrease their reliance on standardized testing. In 2020, UCLA eliminated the standardized testing requirement in their application and saw a 28% increase in applications for freshman seats compared to the previous year. The campus also saw a historic increase in Black applicants, rising 48% over last year, and significant gains across all other racial and ethnic groups: 33% for Latinos, 35% for whites, 22% for Asian Americans, 34% for Pacific Islanders and 16% for American Indians. UCLA campus officials also credited their long years of active recruitment in underserved areas and community partnerships.

The lesson is clear: even if standardized tests are not inherently racially biased, they stand in the way of attracting diverse talent. To be fair, test creators have never claimed to measure drive, resilience or human potential. At most, assessments should be reserved for highly technical roles or to de-risk hiring candidates from another industry.

Also, while we all look for that hospitality gene to make a hiring decision, there is no correlation between a personality type and elite talent even at the front-line. Personality tests that can easily be used to wrongly label people and homogenize workplace cultures should be dropped altogether.

5. "There's already enough diversity in our industry. Let's just steal talent from our direct competitors."

To overturn this orthodoxy, spend time scouting talent in other service industries and testing new platforms.

Conventional wisdom says that with at least four million women and minorities working in U.S. hotels prior to COVID-19, there is enough supply of supervisor-ready talent to source or promote from within the industry to make progress against stated diversity objectives. However, our analysis suggests otherwise: the quality and depth of the diverse talent pool is a significant problem. For example, at the hotel general manager and director levels, including rooms and food and beverage (the two functions that manage the most people and budgets), diversity drops by two-thirds compared to the front-line.

According to our algorithm that uses customer reviews, brand scores and market difficulty to rank the elite talent pool, only 15% of this smaller diverse talent pool are ready to be promoted to these senior property-level positions. In total, we estimate 2,000 to 3,000 minority candidates are ready for promotion from within the hotel industry versus the 10,000 required to fulfill the diversity objectives set by the hotel brands. This does not even factor in the talent needed for the record hotel pipeline which remains largely intact.

Accelerating diversity requires more than increasing pay or incremental innovation. It requires experimentation to identify up-and-coming diverse talent in hotels as well as adjacent industries, schools and communities. Above all, breakthroughs will require new scouting systems and new listening posts. CEOs should make it a higher priority to establish their employer brand where more diverse service leaders can be found. For example, the proportion of Black mid-level managers in retail is 9% compared to 1.6% in U.S. hotels. This is just one example of a more managerially diverse industry that could be tapped by hoteliers to build a more diverse talent pipeline.

The U.S. hotel industry, one of the greatest human meritocracies on earth, is poised for a remarkable comeback but there is much work to be done. In the short term, 5 to 10% of the pre-COVID talent has turned to the gig economy and other industries. A new talent pool must be discovered and accelerated. The industry's ability to improve service and meet its diversity goals will determine the pace of recovery.

Significant innovation in all dimensions of human capital will be required to fend off substitutes like Airbnb and more alternative employers such as Amazon and food delivery apps. Hotel CEOs should begin by developing strategies to overturn orthodoxies and allocate more resources to those courageous enough to do so.

"Any analysis of capital structure should recognize that most balance sheets are dramatically inaccurate because (with the exception of professional sports franchises) they fail to include the value of human capital."

Michael Milliken

6

REPLENISHING AMERICA'S TALENT ENGINE

A merica's most important engine of human meritocracy is facing its biggest challenge ever. A generation of talent is leaving the hotel industry as brands are betting on franchising, delegating human capital management to hundreds of third-party managers who lack an employer brand. Reorganization, incremental improvements, and digitalization of the workplace are necessary but insufficient to fill 3 million annual openings. Radical innovation, supported by innovative technologies, is required to bring the hotel industry's human capital back to equilibrium. It starts with reimagining the role of HR from administrator to the creator of employee-first platforms such as talent marketplaces that advance meritocracy and accelerate diversity. CEOs and Boards of Directors can usher in the new paradigm with deal- making focused on establishing talent exchanges within the hospitality industry and like- minded organizations in adjacent service industries.

● Hotel industry as an engine of meritocracy and growth

Few industries have a track record of generating economic impact and providing upward mobility as hospitality. Overall, immigrants own 29 percent of all restaurants and hotels, more than twice the 14 percent rate for all businesses, according to U.S. census data. Consider the success of people of South Asian origin in the U.S. hotel industry. A majority of these owners are Gujarati, hailing from India, Pakistan, Uganda, and elsewhere. It started in 1942 when a man named Kanjibhai Manchhu Desai left Gujarat, India in search of new opportunities. He was joined by two Gujarati farmworkers, and they took over a 32-room hotel in Sacramento, California, after the property's Japanese-American owner was forced to report to a World War II internment camp. It was far from an overnight success and white competitors, especially in the rural south, put not-very-subtle "American-Owned" signs outside many of their hotels. They gradually expanded by acquiring more properties across states, focusing on the economy segment. By the 1980s, the second-generation kids of these immigrants started expanding the frontiers of their parent's businesses. By 2007, they owned over 21,000 of the 5,2000 hotels in the U.S. or 42% of the market. Furthermore, they have expanded their management companies and launched real estate funds and publicly traded investments in full-service hotel segments in the U.S. in Canada led by Hersha Hospitality Management, Noble Investment Group, Vista Hospitality, and others.

There were two key factors in their success: flexible "handshake loans" between members of the tribe to acquire hotels and reliance on family as a key source of labor.

Once a family purchased a motel, they would live there, and the family members would do all the tasks needed to run it, from cleaning rooms to checking in guests. There are many other examples of how the hospitality industry has created economic opportunity and upward mobility. Refugees from Vietnam and Cambodia first arrived in Orange County by way of Camp Pendleton in 1975. Among them, there was a man named Ted Ngoy who would later be known as the "Donut King." This niche business created an economic pipeline for newly arrived refugees from Cambodia. By the 1990s, there were approximately 1,500 Cambodian- owned doughnut shops in California alone. Unfortunately, it is nearly impossible to replicate the success of these immigrants today, even on a regional scale. This is not because informal sources of capital have dried up, and not due to difficulties with the supply chain or more regulations. It's because costs are prohibitive. Today, most hotel and restaurant chains have divested real estate and are imposing brand standards resulting in higher capital costs and higher fees. Anti-immigration sentiments are adding to a severe labor shortage, unionization is spreading across the service sector and most chains have walked away from their role in developing talent and acting as the lead human capital manager for their respective industries. Consequently, profit margins are being squeezed, capital costs are higher and labor is more expensive and scarce.

● Brutal facts of the hospitality labor markets in 2023

As we enter 2023, hotel operators are on a losing streak in the talent markets. The same industry that has made significant progress over the past decade capturing the customer with direct bookings has lost 20% of its labor market share to other industries. Ironically, these very savvy investors and operators have inadvertently made things worse for themselves by treating HR tech as an afterthought. Most operators continue to invest in advertising and social media on "big tech" 3rd party job sites and ATS platforms that use their funds to grow their own databases and perpetuate control of the talent markets. The good news is that much of this is within the industry's power to change. The first step is to collect facts, analyze the problem's root causes, and quantify the gap between current strategies and the desired outcome. Consider these five brutal facts regarding the labor crisis confronting hospitality operators in the U.S. as we enter 2023:

Fact one: There are currently 1.6 million job openings in U.S. hotels and Quit rates are 2x the national average.

Fact two: U.S. hospitality must hire 2.9 million people a year to reach equilibrium, including 1.3 million replacement hires.

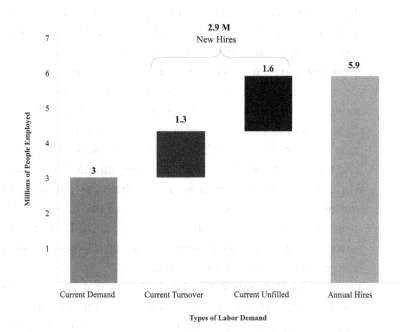

Figure 6.1 U.S. hotel labor market dynamics

Fact three: Even in an optimistic labor market recovery with aggressive recruiting and labor efficiencies, the gap is still 2.4 million.

How can the industry retain and attract sufficient talent to close this shortfall? Consider an optimistic perspective where college graduates with fewer employment prospects join hotels in larger numbers (organic growth), the industry successfully adjusts its labor model to become more flexible, pay more competitive wages and eliminate some positions through efficiencies and service reductions. Let's do the math and see where that takes us.

- **"Bottoms up" organic growth:** Hiring new associate and bachelor's degree college graduates, including hospitality schools. Challenge: even if hotels capture an additional 10% of the entire market of 2 million annual new hires, their turnover is 50%. Number: 100,000 gains with aggressive assumptions that market share is taken from tech, retail, and other sectors that may suffer from a recession and structural changes which reduce the attractiveness of these sectors.
- **Increasing pay to recapture talent:** Capitalizing on the recession and closing the pay gap versus other industries to convince those who have left hospitality to return, including those who work in the Gig economy. Challenge: research says people left for culture, flexibility, and inadequate compensation. There is no evidence that changing compensation alone will work. That said, let's assume hotels increase pay by 20% and owners agree to offer supervisors and above more cash incentives such as profit sharing. Number: 200,000 hiring gains with aggressive assumptions that market share is taken from tech, healthcare, Uber, Airbnb, etc.
- **Efficiencies through digitalization:** Eliminating front-line positions using technology like mobile apps for check-in and consolidating departments such as front desk, housekeeping, and restaurants. Challenge: most jobs and pricing power are in full-service, group, and luxury hotels that require service. Number: 100,000 hiring gains.
- **Attracting talent from other industries hit hard by the recession:** An example is retail, which shed 25,000 in August 2022 alone and continues to shed jobs heading into 2023. Challenge: other than the economy sector, hotels have a mixed record of hiring retail, even in functions such as finance. Training costs are higher than anticipated, and turnover risks are extremely high. Furthermore, delivery and

logistics businesses, including Uber, are growing with average hourly pay, adjusted for taxes, of 2-3X hourly wages in hotels. Number: 100,000 hiring gains.

In conclusion, these optimistic scenarios generate an incremental 500,000 employees. Where does that leave us? Even with the optimistic scenario, the current strategy leaves a gap of 2.4 for the U.S. hotel sector.

Fact four: The top 16 hotel operators are in a class of their own. Almost half of the top 80 largest hotel operators, representing 70% of branded properties, have abysmal talent and diversity scores. We analyzed the quality of talent at the top 80 hotel operators, addressing 12,000 hotels, and developed an algorithm to rank talent, from the frontline employees to General Managers.

$$f(x) = (Service\ Score * w) + (Brand\ Score * w) + (Market\ Score * w) + (Experience\ Score * w) + (Stability\ Score * w)$$

$$Service\ Score\ by\ Department = Service - \left(\frac{Rooms + Location}{2}\right)$$

Brand Score = Brand Prestige by Product Segment [1 (low) and 5 (high)]

$$Market\ Score = (REVPAR\ \Delta\ \%) * Number\ of\ Rooms\ Available$$

Experience Score = Industry Experience

Stability Score = Job Hopping Frequency

We summarized our findings in the Talent Share Matrix Chart that shows a company's share of elite talent on the x-axis and the number of properties managed on the y-axis. We classified high- performing hotel operators from a talent perspective, into two buckets: "High potentials" (talent scores above the median, high growth, and below-average portfolio size and growth) and "Stars" (talent scores above the median, high growth, and above-average portfolio size and growth). A few hotel operators are "Stars" with quality talents that stand above the rest alongside a few notable, small brands and management companies. However, over 50% of the branded hotels are managed by underperforming management companies with below-average talent scores and less than one-star performer per property, whose average tenure is under 24 months. What about progress in diversity, equity, and inclusion? We also ranked the top 80 hotel management companies for diversity – the proportion of elite talent who are women and minorities in their property level supervisor and above ranks over four years (2018-2022). We then performed regression analysis to ascertain the correlation between the quality of talent and diverse elite talent for the same employers. There is a 92% correlation between a change in the company's quality of talent score and its diversity talent score. We analyzed these results by brand segment (i.e., economy vs. luxury), and product type (i.e., resort vs. airport hotel), and the results were within a 10% confidence interval (see Figure 6.2).

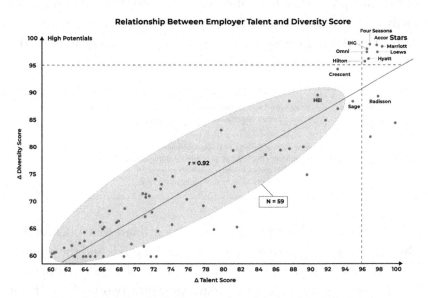

Figure 6.2: Relationship between employer talent and diversity score

If managerial diversity was a performance KPI with equivalent importance to revenue indexes, many of these operators would be out of business. Furthermore, owner-operators – who in theory have the most stakeholder alignment – rank among the worst in DEI. This demonstrates that aside from brands, most of whom are publicly traded or owned by institutional investors, the industry has not made significant strides in diversity at the property management level.

Fact five: Radical innovations – the broader adoption of the hybrid work model, wholesale changes in job qualifications, and a paradigm shift in hospitality recruiting - could generate an additional 1 million talents, closing the labor shortage to 1.4 million.

- **Semi-Qualified "hidden workers":** People with service industry experience who are either unemployed, employed part-time, or have left the workforce and screened out by legacy HR tech due to the flawed recruiting process and ATS filters that require a college degree. Based on a recent Harvard Business School and Accenture study, we estimate the potential gain to be 500,000 people. The challenges include significantly increased recruiting, training, learning, and development costs of 5-10x per employee to $5,000 per year for the front line.
- **Legal immigration:** Qualified hospitality workers such as those trained by hotel chains in countries such as Mexico, the Caribbean, Ukraine, India, and China, where large numbers are seeking to exit. We estimate the potential gain to be 100,000 supervisors and above. The additional costs including visa sponsorship, relocation and housing, assistance with language barriers, cultural adjustment, and other assistance to be $35,000 per employee.
- **Hybrid work models:** People with service industry experience who need to work from home to take care of family or who had intentionally left the hospitality industry to pursue the hybrid work model that is now the norm in other sectors such as technology and professional services. What if the industry changed its labor model to permit finance, accounting, human resources, revenue management, purchasing, and even General Manager to be hybrid? This would also enable department heads and supervisors on the property to demonstrate their leadership potential. We estimate the potential gain, including attracting new talent into the industry, to be 400,000. Additional costs include accelerated training and development,

but there are also potential savings in labor, benefits, and other costs. While they would be expensive and risky, these radical innovations could generate an additional 1 million talents, closing the gap to 1.4 million. There is only one option to close this gap to 500,000 or less: increasing retention to 75%.

● The solution: Building a talent engine of the future

Clearly, addressing the labor/talent crisis in hospitality requires more than stewardship: significant innovation, including new processes and technologies, is needed to increase retention and attract new talent into the industry in parallel. Hotel operators continue to bet on legacy HR tech, including job sites, ATS platforms, and static internal job boards. These passive platforms filter out 80% of "hidden workers" and use generic AI that delivers inaccurate matches. Research also confirms that across industries, internal job boards have failed to advance meritocracy because they are not widely used by over half of women, minorities, and individuals outside a company's privileged social networks.

● What does the future look like?

On the employer side, imagine a Talent Engine actively pulls in individuals who are hidden workers, legal immigrants, and a hybrid workforce. It uses data and algorithms to help organizations identify stars within their organization who are ready to take on the promotion. For example, it may be the Front Office Manager who is ready to be Director of Rooms or that new Director of Rooms you've just hired who outperformed within a brief time and is ready to be a General Manager.

On the talent side, envision employees having fun using the Talent Engine as a portal for learning and development. It becomes their platform for personal branding, accessing career development opportunities, as well as discovering and charting career paths that can be advanced by experiential learning. Talents can showcase their strengths and accomplishments. They can also demonstrate that they are ready for a lateral move or promotion.

Components of a Talent Engine for Service Industries

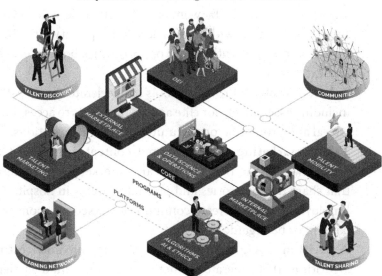

Figure 6.3: Components of a talent engine for service industries

The Talent Engine is powered by AI-powered analytics and includes the following modular components:

- **Data science & operations** – Building scalable solutions to source, rank, and appraise elite talents with leading employers; Writing and testing algorithms that use data science and AI to predict matches between diverse talents and employers in service industries.
- **External marketplace** – Matching diverse supervisors and above talents from service industries with career opportunities at leading hospitality employers; Includes full-time, contract, part-time, and gig opportunities.

- **Internal marketplace** – Matching diverse supervisors and above talents from inside multi- unit organizations with career advancement opportunities, including lateral and promotions, across departments, functions, business units, and geographies.
- **DEI** – Closing the diversity gap by sourcing diverse elite and rising talents - 50% women, 33% minorities, and LGBT supervisors - from within and outside hospitality. Providing diverse candidates with career opportunities both internally and externally.
- **Talent mobility** – Providing tools to accelerate career paths, including assessments for elite and rising talents to access both lateral and promotion opportunities inside organizations.
- **Talent marketing** – Inspirational content, including GM interviews, talent tier awards, and marketing campaigns that share human stories and promote careers in hospitality. Employers can also create communities based on sponsored content or be organic.
- **Algorithms, AI, and ethics** – Developing and testing algorithms that generate predictions of talent rankings, tiers, and matches — using data science to generate employer rankings for the overall quality of talents and DEI by company type, region, and brand segments.
- **Communities/Mentors** – Enabling talents to share their stories, chart career paths, form peers and connections, and engage in hospitality-specific communities both internally and externally, including mentorship, references, and reviews.
- **Talent discovery** – Innovative applications that source hidden workers and talents from outside hospitality, including those outside the traditional workforce, engaging these hidden workers in the external marketplace, learning zone, and communities.
- **Learning network/zone** – Providing a hub for experiential learning, including courses and certificates from leading industry providers and employers, and providing an

empowering platform for user-generated content from industry professionals sharing best practices and innovations.

- **Talent sharing** – Brokering talent exchanges between complementary organizations from different geographies or adjacent industries, including both short-term exchanges and long- term talent-sharing deals, enabling fluid movement of people between business partners.

● Role of AI in providing career pathways:

Finding and matching talents with opportunities is a challenging task for employers. They need to consider various aspects of each talent, such as their skills set, past experience, current role and ranking trend. They also need to understand the specific requirements and expectations of different roles in their industry and how they can be fulfilled by different talents.

This is where industry-specific algorithms add value. These algorithms use both data and theories from the industry to analyze and compare the profiles of talents and roles. They can detect the talents who have the potential and suitability to perform higher level roles, based on their skills, experience and performance. They can also match the talents with the roles that best suit their profile and preferences.

These algorithms also use industry-specific variables to fine-tune their analysis and comparison. These variables are factors that are unique or important for each industry, such as the market demand, the customer satisfaction, the revenue growth, the employee turnover, etc. These variables can affect the performance and potential of both talents and roles in different ways. For example, in the hospitality industry, customer satisfaction is a key variable that can indicate how well a talent or a role is doing in terms of service quality and customer loyalty.

One use case of application of industry specific algorithms is finding and matching talents to a General Manager position at a property level. This position requires a high level of skills, experience and leadership in managing a hotel or a property. The AI matching system can not only find the talents who are already working as General Managers, but also those who have shown their capability to perform the job, such as Assistant General Managers, Hotel Managers and primary directors who report to General Managers at the property level and who have outperformed in their current positions.

The AI matching system can also expand its pool of talents by looking into other industries that have similar or transferable skills and experience to the hospitality industry, such as retail and restaurant industries. These industries also require talents who have skills in customer service, sales, operations, management, etc. The AI matching system can identify the talents who have these skills and experience in retail or restaurant industries and match them with the General Manager position in the hospitality industry. For example, it can find talents who are working as Store Managers or Restaurant Managers in retail or restaurant industries and match them with the General Manager position in the hospitality industry. These talents may have the potential and suitability to perform the job with some training and adaptation.

● The future of Talent Engine

Artificial Intelligence (AI) aims to create machines and systems that can perform tasks that normally require human intelligence, such as reasoning, learning, decision making, and perception. AI can be a powerful tool that can achieve remarkable results when used effectively and ethically. This is especially relevant in the human capital management domain, which is the field of managing the people and talent within an organization. Many industries face challenges in this domain, especially in uncertain times when the business environment and the workforce needs are constantly changing.

The talent ecosystem of the future is a network of interconnected and interdependent actors and entities that collaborate to create value and achieve shared goals. This ecosystem will use data and Artificial Intelligence to improve the processes and outcomes of managing talents, such as finding, growing, keeping, and motivating them, which was hard to do by humans alone.

In the talent ecosystem, talents can utilize the power of knowledge portal, which is a centralized repository of information and resources, to acquire new skills, update their profiles, and access relevant career guidance. The knowledge portal can leverage AI to provide personalized recommendations based on the talent interests, preferences, goals, and current skill level. The knowledge portal can also use natural language processing (NLP) to analyze the employee's queries and feedback, and generate relevant responses or suggestions. The knowledge portal can serve as a one-stop shop for employees to access various learning and development opportunities.

Ultimately, talents can utilize Augmented Reality/Virtual Reality training, which are immersive and interactive learning experiences that can simulate real-world scenarios and challenges. AR/VR training can use AI to adapt the difficulty and content of the training according to the employee's performance and progress. AR/VR training can also use computer vision and speech recognition to capture the employee's gestures and voice, and provide real-time feedback and guidance. AR/VR training can enhance the employee's engagement, retention, and transfer of knowledge and skills in a fun and interactive way.

Talents can also take advantage of learning communities, which are groups of talents who share common interests, goals, or challenges, and collaborate with each other to learn and grow. Learning communities can use AI to facilitate communication, coordination, and collaboration among members. AI can also help identify potential mentors, mentees, peers, or experts who can provide support, advice, or feedback to the talents. Learning communities can create a sense of belonging, trust, and accountability among talents.

The ecosystem also keeps talents engaged and unleashed by using experiential learning, which is a type of learning that involves action, reflection, and application. Experiential learning can use AI to create personalized learning paths for employees based on their skills, career pathways, and preferences. AI can also help match employees with suitable projects, assignments, or gigs that can provide them with hands-on experience and exposure to different roles or functions. Experiential learning can help employees acquire new skills, demonstrate their capabilities, and explore their career options.

Finally, integrating talent activities within the ecosystem with market dynamics is where the power of AI can be felt. Market dynamics are factors that influence the supply and demand of talents and opportunities within the organization. Some of the components of market dynamics are dynamic talent ranking, opportunity matching algorithms, talent worth prediction algorithms and yield management algorithms. Talent ranking on the marketplace is a measure of the talent reputation, performance, and potential on the platform. Talent ranking can use AI to aggregate and analyze data from various sources such as feedback, ratings, endorsements, achievements, and certifications. Talent ranking can help employees showcase their value, attract more opportunities, and access more rewards or incentives. Opportunity matching algorithms are algorithms that use AI to find the best fit between talents and opportunities based on various criteria such as skills, interests, preferences, availability, and location. Talent to opportunity matching algorithms can help them discover relevant opportunities, and help employers find suitable candidates. Talent worth prediction is a prediction of each talent's value or contribution to the organization based on their current skills, performance, and potential. Talent worth prediction can use AI to project the talent's career trajectory, growth rate, and impact. Talent worth prediction can help talents plan their career development, and help employers optimize their talent investment. Yield management is a strategy that aims to maximize the utilization and productivity of talents and opportunities within the organization. Yield management can use AI to monitor and adjust the supply and demand of talents and opportunities based on various factors such as market conditions, seasonality, trends, and events. Yield management can help talents find more opportunities, and help employers allocate resources more efficiently.

A talent ecosystem can benefit both employers and talents, by creating a win-win situation where employers can access the best talents for their needs, and talents can access the best opportunities for their growth. A talent ecosystem can also create a culture of excellence and innovation, where talents are motivated to perform at their highest potential and produce outstanding results.

● The path forward: From steward to market maker

It is widely acknowledged that the hotel industry is not known for R&D or being an early adopter of new technologies. Building a platform where hospitality employees, who represent

300 million worldwide and generate 10% of global GDP, garner recognition and fair compensation for their contribution to the business seems like a daunting task. But the industry is prolific at deal-making and has an impressive track record of integrating new technologies, including reservation systems, channel managers, and loyalty program partners. On the customer side of the service profit chain equation, hoteliers have proven that experimentation is a critical enabler of management processes that build culture. Successful implementation of a Talent Engine similarly requires licensing, integrating, and partnering with many innovative technologies, including start-ups.

The process must be supported by a transformation in the composition and role of the HR function from a "top-down" planner to a facilitator of a "bottoms-up" transparent marketplace that includes internal and external talents.

CEOs and Boards should incentivize internal mobility into HR, which must be seen as part of a larger systems approach to executive talent management. Within HR, there should be roles for brand marketers, strategists, deal makers, and technology integrators. It starts with the realization that one of the most effective ways to promote retention, career ambition, and internal mobility is to champion a free market approach by managers, starting at the highest levels of the corporate organization, and incorporate it into the operating units of the organization, regardless of whether they are managed or franchised. But to do this, it is necessary to change the corporate organizational structure and key management processes of the HR function. The current composition and structure of HR are not set up to innovate.

Rather than a tenure-based appointment like academia, HR executives should have "term limits" like those imposed on certain government offices. "HR should become a passage rite for every senior executive to be a C-suite leader. Departments such as talent acquisition, training and development, compensation and benefits, and organizational learning should require 2–3-year rotations that include the highest-performing directors and VPs from technology, operations, marketing, and other functions, across business units and geographies.

Once corporate HR is reset, the entire corporate office, including strategy, corporate development, finance, and legal, needs to move boldly toward cutting "talent sharing" deals within the industry and with complementary organizations in other service sectors. For example, a hotel brand or operator in part of the industry value chain, such as Extended Stay America (ESA), could develop career paths and exchange talent with a complimentary hotel brand that manages full-service properties, such as Hilton. Talent-sharing exchanges would attract and retain new team members better suited to starting their careers in the budget or limited-service segment and, conversely, those ready to move to full-service or luxury operations. Talent exchanges could also extend into other complementary industries. For example, Hilton could develop a talent exchange platform with Starbucks where its best-in-class regional managers could become food and beverage operators at full-service and luxury hotels. As talent exchanges are implemented in retail, education, and healthcare industries, they could help manage labor supply and demand changes by developing a multi-disciplinary workforce. By partnering with software companies to build a Talent Engine, hospitality leaders can create a virtuous talent cycle: an employer brand that attracts people and strengthens the industry by providing career opportunities, both inside the organization and externally.

By adopting this new perspective, the industry can begin to attract people who are looking for growth and value culture as much, if not more, than compensation. Continuously linking culture, leadership, and mobility can increase the talent pool and retention. The result of these efforts can be an organization that can confidently invest in its people who reach their human potential and become industry leaders themselves.

"I am so excited about Canadians ruling the world."

John Diefenbaker

7

CANADA AS A TOURISM SUPERPOWER

The Canadian economy is at an inflection point. According to OECD forecasts for 2023 to 2034, Canada's GDP will grow at a lackluster annual rate of 1.4%, among the worst performing advanced economies. More recently, Canada has been leveraging its talent pool to develop innovative technology hubs in artificial intelligence and clean energy. Still, although institutions along with tax and immigration policies are working to mitigate Canada's historic "resource curse," those policies have thus far failed to completely break it. The tech sector accounts for $116 billion, or 6% of GDP, while Canada continues to suffer from a gradual loss of global market share in tourism, an underperforming sector that employs twice as many Canadians.

From 1995 to 2019, tourism revenues were stagnant in real dollar terms, ranging from 1.5% to 2.1% of GDP. Tourism played a critical role in Canada's economy prior to the pandemic, accounting for $105.1 billion in revenue for businesses, In 2019, the accommodations segment generated $23.6 billion in revenues and $2.7 billion in operating profits, making hotels the proverbial "cash cow" of the tourism sector.

In 2022-2023, Canadian accommodations and food services (which accounts for 30% of tourism spend) grew at an anemic 3%, employing

1.7 million people (10% of national employment), the same proportion adjusted for inflation as in 1995. The vast majority including small and medium enterprises in tourism are owned and operated by women and minorities, heavily concentrated in Ontario, Quebec, Alberta, and British Columbia.

While domestic travel has recovered, Chinese travel to Canada is down 80% from its peak in 2019, representing a $2.5 billion annual shortfall that has not been offset by a surge in Indian travelers, whose length of stay and spend per trip are lower. Given the long-term geopolitical conflict with China, tensions with India and the expectations of flat growth from U.S. travelers, TD Bank concludes Canadian hospitality spending is unlikely to surpass pre-pandemic levels until at least 2025.

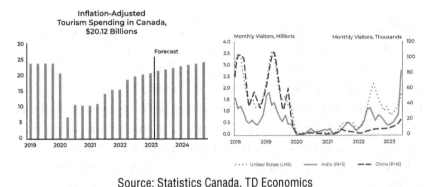

Source: Statistics Canada, TD Economics
Figure 7.1: Canadian hospitality spending and monthly visitors to US, India and Canada

The Canadian economy and the country's position in the world is at an inflection point. Incremental initiatives such as expanded temporary work visas and free trade with India are either stalled or having minimal impact given the unprecedented housing shortage. While investments in artificial intelligence and clean energy show promise, additional growth strategies are required for Canada to realize its potential as an economic power. The largest latent opportunity is to become an environmentally sustainable travel and hospitality superpower in a more turbulent, multi-polar world.

● Key Strategic Issues Facing Canadian Policymakers

In 2019, the federal government released a plan called *Creating Middle Class Jobs: A Federal Tourism Growth Strategy* that started by acknowledging the "Canadian tourism sector was not reaching its potential" and identified "crucial gaps in public and private investment in core tourism assets and attractions." It set a target of increasing the tourism sector's contribution to GDP to top $61 billion by 2030 and improving Canada's ranking in the World Economic Forum's Travel and Tourism Index from 13th in 2021 to 7th by 2030. The report also acknowledged the country needs a "sustained and skilled workforce to propel growth in the sector" but offered no solutions to address the bottleneck other than investing $197.7 million to continue student placement programs. The report pledged $96.5 million to Destination Canada to "promote Canada's brand and assets" and went on to detail a laundry list of priorities, including investing $108 million over three years in the Tourism Growth Program (TGP) $306.8 million in interest free loans for Indigenous businesses, at least $1 billion in revenue generating Indigenous infrastructure projects, and $21 million for building local communities through Arts and Canadian Heritage, all to be coordinated through a Federal Ministerial Tourism Council to "align with international best practices such as those of the United States and France."

The good news is that Canadian policy makers see great economic potential in tourism. The unwelcome news is that Canada is lacking a compelling and differentiated strategy for how to create wealth and jobs in the new travel and hospitality marketplace. Despite spending millions on outside consultants, Ottawa failed to acknowledge that Canadians have lost control of the "cash cow" that is also the most strategic segment of tourism that is also critical to national security: the hotel sector.

Canada's laissez-faire attitude towards the hotel sector for the past decade created a historic opening resulting in a massive invasion of foreign real estate investors, brands, third-party management companies, reservations and property management systems that power these hotels.

Today, there is no Canadian owned hotel brand that is a top choice of hotel owners and developers and is proudly listed on the Toronto Stock Exchange (TSE). The only hotel real estate investment trust (REIT) listed on the TSE is American Hotel Income Properties, which owns limited-service hotels in secondary U.S. markets, managed exclusively by a U.S. hotel management company based in Dallas. Four Seasons shareholders sold the company to foreign private equity firms in 2007. In 2021, Bill Gates' Cascade investment company became majority shareholder of Four Seasons Hotels after the buyout of their former partner, Kingdom Holding Company Affiliate's 23.75% Interest for $2.21 Billion. Four Seasons CEO and most of the management team are no longer Canadian and after losing an underperforming property in Vancouver, Four Seasons *only has 3 properties left in Canada.*

In 2015, Marriott International acquired Delta Hotels from B.C. Investment Management Corporation (who previously acquired the brand from then publicly traded Fairmont Hotels) and assigned the management rights to a third-party operator, JHM. In 2016, Fairmont (once part of Canadian Pacific Corporation) was acquired by France-based AccorHotels, which is partially owned by the government of France and listed on the Paris exchange. Previously, Oxford Properties, the real estate investment subsidiary of the Ontario Municipal Employees Retirement System, purchased seven Canadian Fairmont hotels — including the Banff Springs and Chateau Lake Louise— from Colony Capital and Saudi Arabian Prince Alwaleed bin Talal Abdulaziz for $1.5 billion in 2006, preserving these iconic assets in Canadian control with management contracts subsequently assigned to France based Accor Group.

At present, three U.S. and European hotel chains – Marriott, Hilton and IHG – account for 70% of Canada's 37,359-room hotel development pipeline which is heavily concentrated in producing "cookie cutter" limited-service brands such as Hampton and Holiday Inn in the top 10 Canadian cities.

As in the U.S., Canada's immigrant hotel entrepreneurs are South Asian families, such as the Sunray Group, Easton Group, Silver Hotels and Vista Hospitality who franchise mostly economy and limited-service U.S. and European brands rather than risk investing more equity into deals to create new brands. In contrast, consider a short list the "national champion" hotel chains that are either partially government owned or controlled by Canada's competitors for tourism, the number of hotels in their home country and their respective valuations in $USD as of October 31, 2023: Accor (France/1500 hotels/$8Bn Euronext AC); Intercontinental Hotel Group (U.K./348 hotels/ $11.9Bn LSE); Melia Hotels (Spain/141 hotels/$1.2Bn BME); Group Posadas (Mexico/185 hotels/$731 Million BMV); Lotte (South Korea/30 hotels/$8.5 Bn KRX); Shangri La (Hong Kong/54/$2.3B HKE), Scandic (Sweden/93 hotels/$744 million STO); Dur Hospitality which is partially owned by the Saudi government (Saudi Arabia/32 hotels/$1 billion SSE); Jin Jiang which is 90% owned by the Chinese government (China/8200 hotels/$4.4 Bn SSE); Washington D.C. based Marriott (USA/5,779 hotels/$51.2 billion NYSE), Hilton (USA/5,753 hotels/$37.5 billion NYSE), Choice (USA/6,052 hotels/$5.9 billion NYSE) and New Jersey based Wyndham (USA/6,068 hotels/$5.8 billion NYSE). In addition, private hotel company peers include Hotel Management Japan, Rosewood, Mandarin Oriental (Hong Kong), Peninsula (Hong Kong), Jumeirah (20% owned by the united Arab Emirates), Sandals (Jamaica), Mantra and Crown (Australia), Deutsche Hospitality (Germany), APA Group (Japan), to name a few.

Today, government backed Chinese businesses own over 100 hotels across Canada, including flagship properties branded Fairmont, Delta, Marriott, Hyatt, and Hilton in cities such as Toronto, Quebec City and Vancouver. These properties are managed by foreign management companies that are not accountable to Canadian citizens.

Foreign interest in owning Canadian hotels has a long history, and investors from mainland China, Hong Kong, South Korea, Japan, and the United States have consistently and abundantly extended monetary support to a range of developments in Canada. Offshore investors are interested in Canada for many reasons. For one, there's the stability of the market, both economically and politically. "The Canadian operating environment is very, very strong," says Bill Stone, executive vice-president with CBRE Hotels. "Canada is seen as a very friendly, very secure place to do business."

In 2016, Canada's largest hotel owner and REIT, Innvest, with 81 properties, was acquired by a Hong Kong based investor Bluesky, which is deeply connected to China-based Anbang Insurance Group. The following year saw another foreign investment bump when British Columbia Investment Management Corp. sold its hotel assets, a portfolio of large Canadian hotels including SilverBirch Hotels & Resorts' 26 hotel assets and management operations, to another Hong Kong-based private investor group for $1.1 billion. Other assets controlled by China's biggest property developer Evergrande, whose chairperson is serving a long prison sentence, include the Chateau Montebello, which was acquired from Canada's Oxford properties. It's well established that national governments and businesses use hotel investments around the world for espionage, using a range of methods such as internet connectivity, hidden cameras, electronic intercepts, electronic computer exploitation devices and hacking into property management systems. Several casino hotels in Las Vegas fell victim to cyberattacks in 2023, with MGM suffering a days-long shutdown and Caesars paying over $10 million in ransom. Costar reported that more than a dozen major data breaches have occurred at U.S. hotel chains and management companies since 2010, exposing reservations, credit card data and more. Marriott also confirmed three data breaches since 2018, including one in 2014 which went undetected until 2018, allowing perpetrators to continue accessing data for four years.

Today, with the emergence of Generative AI models, companies become more exposed to cyberattacks every time they are hacked. Hackers can use new AI models, such as WormGPT, to train on the leaked information and generate more accurate and convincing attack emails and contents. These tools can create malicious code, phishing emails, fake websites, or ransomware based on the hackers' data, preferences, and the characteristics of their target victim. These models can also learn from the victims' feedback and responses and adapt their strategies accordingly and ultimately pose a serious threat to companies' and individuals' security and privacy. This is especially true for hotels that rely heavily on human interactions for customer support and other open channels that are prone to social engineering, known as an easy hacking strategy. Therefore, companies need to invest more in digitalizing their processes and building AI-adjacent workforce to reduce the risk of social engineering and other cyberattacks.

After the Chinese firm, Anbang Insurance Group, purchased the Waldorf Astoria in October 2014 for $2 billion. Subsequently, while the Russian President kept his suite at the Waldorf Astoria, the U.S. State department moved its entourage and meetings to other hotels in New York. This marked the end of an era of American diplomacy at the iconic Art Deco midtown hotel. U.S. presidents from Herbert Hoover to Obama have stayed here. Hoover, who lived at the Waldorf Astoria during his retirement, said the luxury hotel's opening in 1931 "marks the measure of a nation's growth in power." More recently, Canadian Security Intelligence Service (CSIS) director David Vigneault appeared on the television show 60 Minutes alongside his peers from the Five Eyes and said: "We have seen in the past acquisition of land, acquisition of different companies where when you start to dig a little bit further, you realize that there is another intent...to acquire locations near sensitive, strategic assets of the country where we knew that the ultimate purpose was for spying operations."

● The Call to Action: Challenges Facing the Canadian Hospitality Industry

Thanks to pent-up demand, inflationary impacts (which benefit hotels given the higher marginal flow through of every dollar of average daily rate to the bottom line), revenues in the Canadian hotel industry are back to pre-covid levels. However, a return to free cash flow generation is more elusive: hotels and restaurants are facing skyrocketing labor, development, and supply costs while customer satisfaction is the lowest in decades. Corporate travel is permanently reduced and according to the Tourism Industry Association of Canada, small business owners are in financial distress with 40% reporting they are likely to cease operations in the next three years due to their inability to pay back Covid loans.

Furthermore, major regions of the country that employ the largest numbers in travel and hospitality such as Vancouver have a severe shortage of hotels with demand exceeding supply by 400,000 room nights. Travel and hospitality contribute $4.4 billion to the Vancouver economy alone and provide 70,000 full time jobs. Prior to the pandemic, British Columbia welcomed 5.5 million international visitors to the province and the industry grew to 19,000 tourism businesses. As a result of the shortage of affordable hotels, Airbnb and other short-term rental platforms are flourishing in British Columbia. However, like the tech industry, the travel industry is expecting a substantial labor shortage in British Columbia in the coming years. Advocates for the provincial tourism industry estimated that there could be a 100,000-person hospitality labor shortage within a decade.

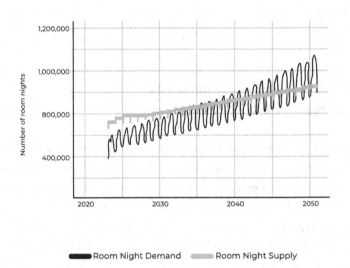

Source: Destination Vancouver, Economic Analysis of Hotel Supply and Projected Demand in Metro Vancouver, 2023 to 2050
Figure 7.2: Hotel Room Night Supply and Demand in Metro Vancouver

In addition to a labor shortage of 300,000 workers, an additional 190,000 (10.9% of accommodation and food service workers) are Temporary Foreign Workers (TFWs). However, these temporary workers have no path to permanent residency and are bound to the employer that brought them into the country until the end of their work permit. According to union representatives and labor relation experts, this makes them reluctant to report abuse. Employers who are dependent on temporary foreign workers are disincentivized to increase wages and improve working conditions.

Canada also faces most of the same diversity, equity, and inclusion issues facing the U.S. hospitality sector: 60.3% of the workforce are women who represent only 14% of property level executives. Canada's hospitality workforce is composed of 30% visible minorities, who represent only 11% of executives at the property executive level and above. Meanwhile, small travel and hospitality businesses that are lauded by policymakers are younger, more innovative, and more likely to be owned by women, minorities, and disabled people with 50% of them classified as immigrant owned and operated. Remarkably, unlike other sectors, almost half of tourism related SMEs started with acquisitions of other businesses and real estate – twice the rate of other SMEs and hence 3 times more likely to require bank and government supported financing. In March 2022, the Business Development Bank of Canada and the Canada Small Business Financing Program had over $4 billion of outstanding financing commitments to tourism with the vast majority to accommodations and food services, 70% of which is earmarked for working capital. Still, this vital segment of the economy continues to struggle. In February 2023, Gloria Loree, the Chief Marketing Officer of Destination Canada told Skift that Canadian tourism businesses are struggling to become profitable: "We are hearing from our hotel owners and tour operators across the country that they're not making as much profit, even though revenue is higher. Their profits are not as high because their labor costs are higher, their supply chain is broken, and food costs are higher."

● Charting a New Strategy for a Sustainable, High Growth Canadian Hotel Sector

Given the historical absence of a strategic policy framework adopted by Ottawa and the lack of foresight by the Canadian capital markets, a paradigm shift is required for Canada to achieve its potential as a hospitality superpower. Growing geopolitical risks and economic turbulence are creating a sense of urgency to reset and forge new partnerships with real estate developers, Canadian banks, private equity, venture capital and foreign sovereign funds to build accommodations and food services sustainably and faster in untapped markets. There are five areas that require addressing: (1) New rules and incentives to create a new generation of work/live Canadian hotel brands; (2) Tax relief for hotel owners and a reallocation of funds from marketing to development; (3) Content requirements for the promotion and protection of Canadian culture, along the same lines as the arts, media, and entertainment industries; (4) The establishment of hospitality and travel hubs in provinces such as Ontario; and (5) the establishment of the equivalent of free enterprise zones for sustainable Indigenous tourism, similar to the Australian model.

The first and highest priority for Canada is to build national brand champions that carry the Canadian flag with assets owned by Canadians. On the development front, the federal government can ensure that domestic hotel ownership and branding are strategic priorities. Ottawa could amend the Canadian Investment Act and mimic its policies in many other sectors that limit foreign ownership of Canadian hotel assets, hotel brands and management companies to 49%. This can be accompanied by new financing and tax incentives for the creation of domestic hotel real estate funds and hotel real estate investment trusts listed on the Toronto Stock Exchange.

The opportunity is much larger than just travel and tourism. Given the new waves of immigration, Canada's persistent housing shortage which has historically been around 100,000 homes annually has increased exponentially and is now over 800,000 homes. In 2022, Canada's population grew by 4.7 people for every housing unit completed the previous year. As New York City's recent initiatives aimed at growing affordable housing suggest, growing the hotel sector and limiting the growth of Airbnb are part of the solution. Extended stay segment hotels, ranging from economy to luxury, are one of the solutions that could close the housing shortage gap without less risks of cyclicality or seasonality. In Asia, branded service apartments that also function as hotels are the single most successful real estate class and global growth in the extended stay hotel ("work/live") segment is forecasted to triple from $54 billion to $166.58 billion dollars between 2023-2033, but Canada's share of the global pipeline is anemic.

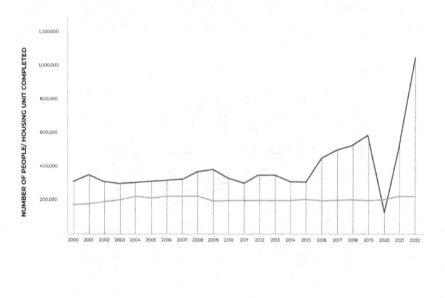

Population Growth   Housing Completion

Source: Fraser Research, Canada's Growing Housing Gap Comparing
Population Growth and Housing Completions in Canada, 1972–2022
Figure 7.3: Canada Population Growth vs Housing Completion

Sustainable hotel brands that use artificial intelligence and advance Indigenous tourism should also be added to the eligibility list for innovation grants, loans, and innovation funds such as the C$7 billion Strategic Innovation Fund (SIF). In addition to extended stay products, developers can focus on sustainable luxury brands and bespoke, small-scale sustainable tourism that provides an alternative to mass market travel and advances culture, art, local craftsmanship and the Indigenous understanding of the environment. These experiences will be constructed with the environmental and spiritual knowledge of Indigenous communities and their entrepreneurs.

Second, the Canadian hotel industry needs tax relief. Canadian travelers and their international guests also pay approximately $4 billion in annual taxes collected by various levels of government.

For the industry to grow, this 7-15% tax burden on the hotel sector (including federal, provincial, municipal and destination Canada resort fees) must be rationalized in exchange for hotels eliminating resort and other junk fees.

Source: Meanwhile in Canada Facebook Account
Figure 7.4: Canada Tourism Memes

This would free up $1 billion in equity capital that will be reinvested into growing the sector to develop new destinations and brands that replace centralized, government led marketing. Hundreds of millions are being wasted in cliché destination marketing that doesn't generate a return and has made Canada the subject of funny memes and other jokes on social media.

This redistribution of wealth from government coffers to small and medium enterprises could lay the groundwork for Canada's institutional investors such as Canadian pension funds, private equity firms and debt investors to "pile in" and co-invest in Canadian hotel companies and sustainable tourism developments and rely less on the U.S. for their investment returns.

Third, federal and provincial governments could legislate Canadian content requirements which have successfully protected cultural heritage and provided a platform for home-grown Canadian talent in other industries. As other governments have demonstrated content requirements, hospitality must address human capital: General Managers must be Canadian residents. Citizens or skilled refugees and the front-line workforce may be developed along the lines of the "Saudization" initiative that aims at reducing dependence on expatriate hospitality managers and employing more youth, with a renewed spirit for making a positive social impact on local communities.

It would be advisable that hospitality programming content requirements be like songs on the airwaves that require at least two of the following conditions to be met – music, artist, performance, and lyrics (MAPL) – to be Canadian. On the media front, the Canadian Radio-television, and Telecommunication Commission (CRTC) presently requires that at least 55% of all programming aired annually by broadcast television stations, and at least 50% of programming aired daily from 6:00 pm to midnight must be Canadian content. If it weren't for the CRTC, Drake, The Weekend and Bryan Adams would have been undiscovered. Canadian content rules helped Celine Dion get big enough to have multiple residencies in Las Vegas but there are few if any Canadian made celebrity chefs with venues in Las Vegas.

Canadian hospitality content requirements must go beyond furniture, fixtures and equipment and encompass food and beverage suppliers and a comprehensive range of technologies including online travel agencies, reservations, and customer relationship management software as well as human resource technologies such as applicant tracking systems and job sites. These marketplaces should be facilitated by industry associations and require a certain percentage of suppliers be First Nations business owners.

Fourth, provincial governments can engage industry stakeholders to develop strategies to establish hospitality hubs around hotels, schools, and tech centric universities such as University of Guelph and Waterloo, Ontario. The Business Development Bank of Canada (BDC) could back angel and VC investments that develop new human capital technology platforms to address the number one problem cited by Canadian SMEs in hospitality and tourism: recruiting and training skilled employees by using artificial intelligence, virtual and augmented reality to scale experiential learning programs.

The economies of scale in production and learning provided by having a geographic cluster for tourism and hospitality are not the only objectives. Canada's recent experience with Meta and Google - who refused to pay local news content providers and blocked and subsequently left the Canadian market - is a risk that the Canadian travel industry should never face. A cluster that includes start-up incubators in hospitality provides fertile grounds for (1) developing Canadian based online travel agencies that can reduce the country's dependence on foreign big tech reservation systems and booking engines and offer curated local experiences similar to what C-trip has done in China for domestic travelers and (2) new collaborative gig work platforms that promote the active participation of Indigenous people as entrepreneurs who can engage in project based work including artisan manufacturing and luxury craftsmanship.

Fifth, a bolder growth strategy does not require abandoning Canada's "true north," which is aligning the visitor economy with climate change goals to achieve net-zero emissions by 2050. These goals cannot be met without regulating the real estate industry and creating incentives for stakeholders to self-regulate their practices. Hotels and resorts are among the worst polluters of any industry on earth and create 1.9 billion pounds of waste each year (enough to fill 37 million suitcases), use 3.9 billion gallons of water each year (equal to one person taking a shower nonstop for 277 years) and use 84.7 billion kwh each year (enough energy to power 64.5 million television sets). Global hotel chains have announced goals to reduce emissions, but those superficial pledges have remained, if not entirely, focused on operational carbon via reductions in fossil fuel use, waste, and water usage and not on construction. With no real definition of net zero, hotels can easily obtain meaningless certifications such as those from LEED, that falsely inform travelers of their sustainability practices. Embodied carbon, the term that encapsulates all the harmful greenhouse gasses emitted *during renovation and construction of a building*, remains an outsized part of any hotel project's footprint. Embodied carbon in hotel related construction contributes to at least 21% of global emissions compared to only 1% for hotel operations. According to hospitality journalist, Jackie Caradonio, the hotel industry's definition of net-zero carbon emissions is subject to obfuscation and is therefore "a big lie." Since 2019, Statistics Canada followed UN guidelines, measured energy use and Greenhouse Gas (GHG) emission attributable to tourism, which represents 6.1% of energy use (711,740 terajoules of energy), 3x their GDP contribution and 6.4% of Canadian GHG (50,274 kilotonnes), with hotels representing 3.2% energy and 2.8% of GHG. However, these figures are misleading because they don't include construction and development. Therefore, the hotel industry, in particular developers and owners, are not held accountable for the lion's share of their impact on the environment.

The first project in North America that significantly advanced sustainability through reduced embodied carbon was the Citizen M in Los Angeles, which featured the latest modular approaches that employ parametric prefabrication, allowing for flexible outputs, reducing supply chain costs, and reducing construction waste to just 2%, down from 10-20% for a traditionally built project.

The experience of the United Arab Emirates, a country with a desert landscape that has managed to turn from a modest fishing village into a diversified economy that counts hospitality as 21.3% of GDP and ranks third in the world in sustainable development is a relevant case study for Canada. It is also worth drawing attention to the transformation of Saudi Arabia, which is developing sustainable tourism and digital technologies as part of an innovative and bold Vision 2030. For example, the Red Sea project, launched in 2017, promotes luxury tourism and includes an archipelago of 90 islands on the west coast of Saudi Arabia and the coast of Tabuk province. The massive project aims to attract international tourism to the pristine islands, create up to 70,000 jobs, and protect the Red Sea ecosystem. In accordance with the stated goals of Red Sea Development, it is necessary to produce, store and use 100% of energy from renewable sources on site. The company, which offers private tours along the Red Sea coast, plans to become the largest certified nature reserve where light pollution is prohibited.

In contrast, Canada does not have a systematic approach to the broad-scale development of a sustainable tourism and hospitality industry. In the meantime, appropriate projects could contribute to the creation of many jobs as well as the gentrification of territories and the inclusion of Indigenous people in the active workforce, contributing to social equality and reducing the digital divide. Indigenous tourism – businesses majority owned, operated and/or controlled by First Nations, Metis or Intuit peoples that demonstrate a connection and responsibility to the traditional territory where it operates – has seen a steady growth in Canada in recent decades. From 2002 to 2015, *the number of Indigenous travel companies almost doubled from 892 to 1,500,* their contribution to GDP increased from $600 million to $1.4 billion, and the number of employees increased from 13,000 to 33,000 people representing $870 million dollars in wages and salaries and $67 million in consumption tax revenues.

Some dashed industry expectations aside, there's reason for optimism, according to Canada's tourism leaders. The sector will receive $1 billion for 2022-2023 while the government develops a new national tourism growth strategy in collaboration with the industry. In addition, Canada's Indigenous tourism sector will receive $20 million from a first-ever dedicated Indigenous Tourism Fund plus $4.8 million to support the Indigenous Tourism Association of Canada over a two-year period, which represents a longer-term commitment than last year.

The potential is evident, but progress will require overturning orthodoxies or deeply held beliefs at the highest level of both the public and private sector. According to a 2018 survey, cultural tourism is seen as a priority by more than 60 percent of the 286 Indigenous tourism operators which took part in the survey. The respondents "most frequently identified access to financing and marketing support and training as their most desired supports for business development and growth." Nunavut's operators, for example, highlighted training, infrastructure, reputation, and opportunities for youth as being equally important for them. Thus, a flexible and diverse approach is needed in development and implementation of appropriate strategies, programs, and concrete steps. The case studies of Norway's transformation of the cruise industry and indigenous tourism in the Barrier Reef region of Australia provide insights into why Canadians need to think bigger.

● Case Study: Norway's EV Powered Cruise Industry

Norway is leading the way in the adoption of low- and zero-emission vehicle technologies in the cruise industry. In 2015, the first fully electric ferry, the MF Ampere, started operating in Western Norway. The Norwegian government subsequently implemented its Climate Plan 2021–2030, to advance sustainable transportation. By 2030, it hopes to cut emissions from domestic maritime transportation in half compared to 2005 levels. The decarbonization initiative implemented in Norway may have significant global ramifications. For almost 250 operational ferry and high-speed vessel connections, low- or zero-emission solutions have been evaluated or are being examined. Green policies have been fast-tracked. A resolution passed by the Norwegian Parliament calls for the elimination of emissions from ferries and cruise ships operating in the West Norwegian Fjords, specifically the World Heritage Sites of Geirangerfjord and Naerøyfjord, by 2026 at the latest. The fjords will thus be among the first zero emission maritime zones in the world. Proposals have also been made to amend the regulations on environmental safety for ships and mobile offshore equipment. A carbon tax of 2,000 NOK per ton by 2030 is also part of the plan, along with low- and zero-emission criteria for ferries starting in 2023 and high-speed ferries starting in 2025.

Today, the Norwegian company Hurtigruten, whose fleet includes 17 ships, is not only the largest, but also the greenest operator of expedition cruises in the world. The company has been operating ships with hybrid engines for several years, and now it is going to go even further. In 2019, a new step at Hurtigruten was the bunkering of cruise ships with liquefied biogas, the raw materials for which are fish processing waste and other organic waste. Hurtigruten recently revealed that its first net zero cruise ship will be ready by 2030, ahead of plans to decarbonize the whole fleet. The 443-foot-long, 270-cabin edition of the zero-emission ship can accommodate 500 passengers and 99 crew members. The new ship will also feature a cargo hold and transport automobiles because the company has been shipping freight along Norway's coast for 130 years. Norwegian business Northern Xplorer, which recently launched its new concept cruise ship, the MM 130, is showcasing yet another environmentally sensitive design. The concept cruise ship, the first of a planned fleet of 14, was created with the environment's influence as a top priority. The ship is equipped with solar, wind, and solar power, hydrogen fuel cell technology, electric propulsion, and rechargeable battery systems. In addition, the ship will produce its own clean fuel, making it self-sufficient.

Norwegian companies Magnora ASA, Prime Capital and Troms Kraft are also creating a plant for the large-scale production of green hydrogen, which will then be processed into green ammonia for use as marine fuel. The project is being implemented in Tromsø, the largest city in Norway beyond the Arctic Circle. Fuel production is expected to begin in 2025. Norway also has the potential to become a world leader in biogas production because its strong fish processing and wood processing sectors can provide large volumes of organic waste. When it comes to sustainability, Norway is a setting the global benchmark with its innovative approaches, including public-private partnerships that address not just the tourism industry but the entire ecosystem as a whole.

● Case Study: Great Barrier Reef Indigenous Tourism (Australia)

Australia generates 3.5% of its GDP ($60 billion) from tourism, which is significantly bigger than Canada's figures despite a population that is 30% smaller, in part because of its coherent execution of a well-developed strategy with respect to Indigenous travel. In 2022, Australians spent more than $3 billion on First Nations tourism activities, alongside $1.3 billion by over 1.4 million international visitors.

The process of creating Indigenous tourism hubs started in Australia, which has since developed the equivalent of special enterprise zones in Cairns and the Great Barrier Reef for sustainable tourism. The Indigenous Innovation and Entrepreneurs Program (IIEP) was open (and continues to function) to Indigenous businesses, innovators, or entrepreneurs across all industries, with an increased focus on the participation of Indigenous tourism operators.

Opening in January 2020, the Cairns Indigenous Tourism Hub provides a location for four independent tourism-related businesses, each operating separately but complementing each other. The businesses are: AppOriginee, an Indigenous experience booking platform; the K'gari 3 Sisters Art Gallery and Gift Shop; GumbuGumbu Bugang Bulmba, a restaurant serving bush food made from locally sourced native ingredients; and Indigenous Tours, established to develop tourism products in partnership with local Indigenous groups. The Hub also provides office space for the Gimuy Walubara Yidinji Elders Aboriginal Corporation and a meeting place for Elders in the local Cairns community. There are strong efforts to integrate Indigenous cultural values into the tourism industry. Moreover, an active and engaging social media presence is encouraged. Also, the need to strengthen relationships between traditional owners and mainstream tourism businesses is emphasized.

Today, millions of Australians are now sharing their Indigenous cultural tourism experiences through the posting of their photos and stories with a destination hashtag. The value co-creation idea comes from the notion that consumers will play a critical role not just in marketing and content distribution but in the design of new experiences and products to make sure that educational value is added from the consumer's point of view. The value for the luxury consumer lies in the educational experience gained. In turn, socially sustainable luxury tourism could also empower life-sustaining activities for remote communities on a global scale if informed by Indigenous cultural governance to facilitate sustainable tourism. The first step is for Canadians to take back control of their hotel industry, establish new forms of business-government cooperation, and take bolder steps to become "first among nations" in global hospitality.

熟能生巧。
Pinyin: shú néng shēng qiǎo.
English: Experience can breed skill.
Key Vocabulary:
熟 (shú) — experience, practice
巧 (qiǎo) — skill; skilled; timely
Though some people are naturally gifted, the truth is that practice makes perfect.

MOUGULAN SEEKING EXTRAORDINARY TALENT IN CHINA

《进入中国市场：疫情过后，
美国商界领袖进驻中国要考虑的八大经验》

The U.S. and China are in the Early Stages of a Protracted Economic War. In 2015, I attended a private lecture at the Harvard Club in Shanghai, hosted by Harvard Business School professor Warren McFarlan following his book, <u>Can China Lead? Reaching the Limits of Power and Growth</u>. In his book, Professor McFarlan argued that China did not have the cultural or soft power to replace the U.S. as a superpower. At the time I was CEO of a China based hospitality company and asked a few of my Chinese executives to attend the briefing. Every country has its own propaganda and I was interested in their perspectives, especially after we toured the Korean War museum in Seoul. To my surprise, they shared an entirely different history about the Korea war with Americans as the initial aggressor as widely taught in Chinese public schools.

美国和中国正处于一场旷日持久的经济竞争的早期阶段。2015年，我参加了上海哈佛俱乐部(Harvard Club)举办的一次私人讲座，由哈佛商学院（Harvard Business School）教授沃伦·麦克法兰(Warren McFarlan)主持，讲座的主题是他的著作《中国能领导吗？达到权力和增长的极限》(Can China Lead? Reaching the Limits of Power and Growth)。McFarlan教授在书中指出，中国不具备取代美国成为超级大国的文化或软实力。当时我担任一家中国公司的首席执行官，并邀请几位中国高管参加了一次讨论会。每个国家都有自己的政治宣传，我对中国高管们的观点很感兴趣，尤其是在我们参观了首尔的朝鲜战争博物馆之后。中国人与美国人对同一段战争历史，有完全不一样的认知，中国的历史课本说美国人是最初的侵略者，这与中国的公立学校广泛传授的观点大相径庭。

Professor McFarlan was not an ordinary professor: he earned three degrees from Harvard, wrote over 300 cases and served six years as co-director at the Case Development Center at the Tsinghua University School of Economics and Management in Beijing, a post co-funded by the CEO of largest U.S. based private equity firm Blackstone Group. His book was not even published in China but had the courage to share his views in private with HBS alumni working in Mainland China. In his presentation, McFarlan characterized China as "a culture of engineers," with exceptional capabilities in infrastructure and manufacturing, constrained in a country whose state -owned enterprises and government institutions were fundamentally incapable of an equivalent transformation. McFarlan did not underestimate the rise of the capitalist class in China and the appeal of its Mercantilist model – which was based on replicating Singapore's success by creating economic enterprise zones. Indeed, China's path to state-led capitalism was well-researched and methodical and modeled after the East Asian Tigers, especially Singapore. However, if China could not lead, the implications were not good: it would either fall apart like the Soviet Union, gradually democratize and play by our rules or its immaturity on the world stage would result in World War three or its equivalent. It was not surprising that my Chinese colleagues brushed aside McFarlan's research as culturally biased, short-sighted, and self-serving.

McFarlan教授并不是一位普通的教授：他在哈佛大学获得了三个学位，撰写了300多个案例，并在北京清华大学经济与管理学院案例开发中心，担任了6年的联合主任，该职位由美国最大的私募股权公司百仕通集团（Blackstone Group）首席执行官共同出资。McFarlan教授的书甚至没有在中国出版，但他有勇气私下与在中国工作的哈佛商学院校友，分享自己的观点。在他的演讲中，McFarlan教授将中国称为"工程师的文化"，因为在这个国家，在基础设施和制造领域具有卓越的能力，但受到国有企业和政府机构根本无法进行等价转型的国家的限制。McFarlan教授并没有低估中国资本主义阶级的崛起及其模式的吸引力，这种模式的基础是通过创建经济企业区，来复制新加坡的成功。事实上，中国的资本主义之路，是经过深入的研究且有条不紊进行的，并以东亚四小龙为榜样。然而，如果中国不能发挥领导作用，那后果将不容乐观：要么像苏联那样解体，逐渐民主化，按西方规则行事；要么在世界舞台上继续"不成熟"，这将导致第三次世界大战。我的中国同事对McFarlan教授的研究不屑一顾，认为他的研究带有文化偏见，目光短浅，这并不奇怪。

In contrast, Harvard Professor William Kirby, a Sinologist by training, recently characterized the U.S-China relationship as a marriage rather than a rivalry. Kirby said the U.S. and China *are basically married: when one of us rolls over, the other falls.*" He has a point. There is no doubt that the economic relationship between the U.S and China remains the world's most important: China holds $1.2 trillion of U.S. Treasuries and nearly $700B in goods and services were sent between China and the United States in 2019. U.S. exports to China create 2 million jobs in sectors such as services, higher education, agriculture and capital goods such as airplanes and semiconductor devices. The service sector, which includes financial services, travel, media, and technology, is over 52% of China's GDP (versus 67% for the U.S). The children of this marriage of convenience include the millions of Chinese students educated at top U.S. universities and they needed the parents to behave like grown-ups.

相比之下，接受过汉学家训练的哈佛大学教授威廉·柯比（William Kirby），最近将中美关系描述为婚姻而不是竞争。柯比（Kirby）说，中国和美国"基本上是一段婚姻关系：当一方跌倒时，另一方也会不顺。"他说的很有道理。毫无疑问，中美之间的经济关系仍然是世界上最重要的：中国持有1.2万亿美元的美国国债，2019年中国和美国之间的商品和服务贸易额，接近7,000亿美元。美国对中国的出口在服务、高等教育、农业以及飞机和半导体设备等资本产品领域，创造了200万个就业岗位。服务业，包括金融服务、旅游、媒体和科技等领域，占中国GDP的52%以上（美国为67%）。这段"婚姻"的子女，包括数百万在美国顶级大学接受教育的中国学生，他们需要父母像成年人一样行事。

It turns out, they were both right. According to state media, president Xi told president Trump in a phone call in March 2020, that US-China relations had reached an "important juncture". Working together brings both sides benefits, fighting hurts both. Cooperation is the only choice," he said. Xi hoped the US would take "substantive actions" to improve US-China relations to develop a relationship that is "without conflict and confrontation" but based on "mutual respect and mutually beneficial cooperation."

事实证明，双方都是对的。据官方媒体报道，习近平主席在3月底的一次电话中，告诉特朗普总统，中美关系已经到了一个"重要关头"：合则共赢，斗则俱伤。合作是唯一的出路。习近平主席希望美国采取"实质性行动"改善中美关系，发展一种"无冲突，无对抗"，但基于"相互尊重，互利合作"的关系。

It was too late. The truth is that it was a rocky marriage to begin with and it's now over. And the couple are on unbelievably bad terms, both behaving irrationally with a high barrier digital war growing taller by the day, separating their civilizations. It is not the purpose of this writer to place blame on China, international organizations, or the U.S. for economic destruction and social dislocation caused by the pandemic. The bigger issue for global business leaders and their stakeholders is what is next and how global brands can survive and perhaps even capitalize on the decoupling with China.

Perhaps the inflection point was not a digital war with Huawei or the Coronavirus. It was when CCTV and Tencent turned off the NBA, which had 500 million Chinese viewers, after a single tweet from a team owner supporting the Hong Kong protestors. Beijing's disproportionate response to a tweet and the NBA's inability to engage in business diplomacy to overcome this incident and reinstate the single most popular sport in China was a clear signal that we were in a cultural war.

但已经太迟了。事实上，这段婚姻一开始就不稳定，而现在也已经结束。这对"夫妇"的关系糟糕得难以置信，两人的行为都不理性，随着网络骂战的日益高涨，两国的"文明"也被分割开来。本文作者的目的并不是将疫情造成的经济破坏和社会混乱归咎于中国、国际组织或美国。对于全球商业领袖及其股东而言，更大的问题是下一步该做什么，以及全球品牌如何在与中国的脱钩过程中生存，甚至可以获利。

或许转折点不是有关华为或冠状病毒的网络之争。而是当中央电视台和腾讯视频，选择封锁拥有5亿中国观众的NBA节目，原因是球队老板发了一条支持香港抗议者的推特文。北京方面对一条推特的不当回应，以及NBA无法通过商业外交手段来解决此事件并恢复中国最受欢迎的体育项目，都是一个明确的信号，表明我们正处于一场"文化革命"之中。

So, what does this mean for business leaders aspiring to build global brands in hospitality, retail, and other service sectors? Will Chinese consumers still seek American brands and content? Or will government initiatives push them towards alternatives? How can business leaders create value in the 2nd largest economy in the world which plays by a different set of rules? Is it time to exit or double down? Should aspiring global brands even consider entering China in the 2020s and beyond?

那么，这对于那些渴望在酒店业、零售业和其他服务领域，打造全球品牌的商界领袖来说，意味着什么呢？中国消费者还会追求美国的品牌和产品吗？或者中国政府的举措会将他们推向其他选择？中国作为世界第二大经济体，商界领袖们如何在遵循不同规则的情况下创造价值？是该退出还是加倍下注？品牌甚至应该考虑进入中国市场吗？

Category-leading U.S. brands appear committed to the China market, less for the supply chain but more for a significant portion of their revenues, growth, and innovation. While the media likes to cover the supply chain, one thing continues to save the marriage from a bitter divorce: the Chinese consumer. Consumer interests are continuing to converge as tech savvy Chinese millennials are seeking the latest brand innovations. Pfizer, Apple, Nike, the NBA, Proctor and Gamble, Starbucks, KFC, Wyndham, Disney, General Motors, Intel, and Microsoft are the agents of social impact and have spent decades investing in China where they are perceived as top employers. They are not surely going to walk away from doing business in China.

领先的美国品牌，似乎更关注中国市场，而不是中国供应链，更关注中国市场的营收、增长和创新。虽然媒体喜欢报道有关供应链的话题，但有一个因素仍在继续挽救这桩婚姻：那就是中国的消费者。随着精通科技的中国千禧一代寻求最新的品牌创新，消费者的兴趣正在不断趋同。辉瑞（Pfizer）、苹果（Apple）、耐克（Nike）、NBA、宝洁（Proctor and Gamble）、星巴克（Starbucks）、肯德基（KFC）、温德姆（Wyndham）、迪斯尼（Disney）、通用汽车（General Motors）、英特尔（Intel）、微软（Microsoft）和领英（LinkedIn）等公司，都是社会影响的推动者，他们已经投入数十年的时间在中国进行投资，并被视为顶尖雇主，他们无疑不会轻易退出中国市场。

It is not just the size of the Chinese market or the growth story that remains attractive to these companies. The key advantages for China have been its relative ease of doing business and its cutting-edge infrastructure. But now it is their world class talent in science, engineering, Artificial Intelligence and more. As large markets go, there are no alternatives to create shareholder value through innovations that can become global anywhere near China.

对这些公司来说，具有吸引力的不仅仅是中国市场的规模。中国的主要优势，是相对容易的经商环境和先进的基础设施。但现在，他们拥有世界一流的科学、工程和人工智能等领域的人才。就大型市场而言，在中国附近没有其他地方可以通过创新来创造股东价值，使其在全球范围内实现。

Despite all the hype about the new "Indo-Pacific," India, which is turning into a one-party religious state, is not yet a viable alternative. Consider this list of companies that have exited one-sided joint venture deals in India after failing to open factories and stores on a meaningful scale, in the past few decades: Walmart, Hilton, IBM, General Motors, and DKNY to name a few. India is at least a decade behind on artificial intelligence and still suffers from its hangover from 200 years of colonization with massive bureaucracy, high tariffs, poor infrastructure, ethnic and religious strike.

印度正在变成一个一党专政的宗教国家，这不是一个可以取代中国的地方。看看过去几十年在印度退出单边合资协议的公司名单：沃尔玛（Walmart）、希尔顿（Hilton）、IBM、通用汽车（General Motors）和DKNY等等。印度仍然遭受着200年殖民统治遗留下来的问题：官僚作风庞大、高关税、基础设施差和安全隐忧。

Moreover, India is playing its old game of balancing Russian and Chinese interests with their American friends. China's low-cost mobile phone company Xiaomi is India's market leader and China is investing at least $15 billion a year into Indian companies in sectors such as pharmaceuticals. China also has its eyes on the big Indian prize: infrastructure.

The bottom-line is American companies have never succeeded in India. Now China is ahead of the curve in India. Even if China Inc falters, India is at least 50 years away from being an alternative to China for anything except raw talent acquisition in Computer Science, education and healthcare.

此外，印度正在玩一个平衡中国和美国朋友利益的老游戏。中国的低成本手机公司小米，在印度市场具有领先地位，中国每年向印度制药等行业的公司投资至少150亿美元。中国也将目光投向了印度最大的"奖项"：基础设施建设。

归根结底，美国公司从未在印度取得成功。现在，中国在印度领先一步。即使中国步履蹒跚，但除计算机科学和医疗保健领域的人才输出以外，印度还需要至少50年的时间才有可能取代中国。

Consider the success of these American based companies in China:

Biopharma: Pfizer is China's market leader in cardiovascular and antibiotics and has invested $1.5B in China and is the country's leading foreign biopharmaceutical company with four state of the art manufacturing plants and 11,000 employees in over 300 cities.

Sports: NBA China, the separate company the league set up in 2008 to manage its retail deals with Alibaba and a 5 year $1.5B content deal with Tencent, is now valued by the league at $10-15 billion. The league has offices in Beijing, Shanghai, Taipei and Hong Kong, and nearly 500 million fans watched NBA programming on Tencent during the 2018-19 season and 21 million fans watched Game 6 of the 2019 Finals, according to NBA data. The league also has more than 200 million followers on social media in China. In March, the league opened the second-largest NBA store outside of North America in Beijing. Despite their current challenges, the NBA's success in building the game in China is remarkable.

看看这些美国公司在中国取得的成功：

生物制药行业：辉瑞（Pfizer） 公司是中国心血管和抗生素市场的领导者，在中国投资了15亿美元，是中国市场领先的外国生物制药公司，拥有4家最先进的制造工厂，在300多个城市拥有1.1万名员工。

体育运动行业：NBA中国（NBA China），该联盟于2008年成立，是一家独立的公司，用以管理其与阿里巴巴（Alibaba）的零售业务，以及执行与腾讯（Tencent）达成的一项为期5年、价值15亿美元的内容协议。目前该联盟的估值为100亿至150亿美元。NBA在北京、上海、台北和香港，均设有办事处，根据NBA的数据显示，在2018-2019赛季期间，近5亿球迷在腾讯的平台上，观看了NBA的节目，2,100万球迷观看了2019年总决赛的第六场。该联盟在中国社交媒体上的粉丝超过2亿。今年3月，联盟在北京开设了北美以外第二大的NBA门店。 尽管目前面临诸多挑战，但NBA在中国打造篮球运动的成功令人瞩目。

Retail: Walmart, who committed $1.2B to build distribution and logistics across China in 2019 recently confirmed it is proceeding with investing $425mm in Wuhan in the next 5-7 years to open at least four new Sam's Club stores, 15 additional shopping malls, and more community stores in the capital of China's Hubei province. The U.S.-based retailer already has 34 stores and two distribution centers in the city.

零售行业：沃尔玛（Walmart）承诺在2019年斥资12亿美元，在中国各地建设配送和物流业，最近证实，沃尔玛将在未来5-7年在武汉投资4.25亿美元，在中国湖北省省会开设至少4家Sam's Club商店、15家额外购物中心和更多社区商店。这家总部位于美国的零售商，在该市已有34家门店和两个配送中心。

Hospitality: Wyndham is China's largest foreign hotel franchisor with over 1500 properties under six brands and expects to open 500 more hotels in the next 3 years. Starbucks, which has over 4200 stores in China generated an estimated $2.9B in revenues, remains committed to investing $130mm USD to launch a global roasting facility in its coffee innovation park.

休闲服务行业: 温德姆 (Wyndham) 集团是中国最大的外资酒店特许经营商，拥有六个品牌1,500多家酒店，并计划在未来3年内，再开设500多家酒店。星巴克 (Starbucks) 在中国拥有4,200多家门店，收入估计达29亿美元。星巴克 (Starbucks) 仍致力于投资1.3亿美元，在其中国的咖啡创新园 (coffee innovation park) 设立全球烘焙设施。

Education: U.S. universities looking for lost revenues after Covid-19 will continue to seek out Chinese students. Chinese students studying in the U.S. grew from 100,000 in 2009 to almost 400,000 in 2018, generating a significant source of revenue for universities and colleges. Furthermore, while their numbers have slightly shifted to the U.K. and Canada, according to Professor Kirby, this is an opportunity to improve marriage: "these are our children. What we need now are some really grown up parents."

教育行业: 在Covid-19疫情过去之后，美国大学为了弥补损失的收入，将会继续招收中国学生。在美国留学的中国学生，从2009年的10万人，增长到了2018年的近40万人。这些中国学生为美国的学校，创造了可观的收入。此外，根据柯比教授 (Professor Kirby) 的说法，这是一个改善婚姻的机会:"这些是我们的孩子。我们现在需要的是一些真正'成熟'的父母。"

● The Game is Changing and It's a Great Opportunity for New Entrants

游戏规则正在改变，这对新玩家来说是一个巨大的机会

Nevertheless, the legacy American brands that built their businesses in China over the last several decades are going to face significant challenges in the 2020s. In the coming years, new local upstarts will emerge, and their brands will fall out of favor with the Chinese consumer. The incumbents who view the Chinese market as a source of innovation will survive. A new generation of category leaders can seize the day and build profitable domestic businesses in China.

For these reasons, Mogul Hospitality, the venture I founded in 2019 is entering the Chinese market. Our mission is to empower hospitality employees in China and grow the talent pool in the context of a record hotel pipeline. We are also focusing our local community initiatives on recognizing the 30 million migrant workers, mostly mothers who comprise nearly one-third of China's hotel labor market and live apart from their families, with an annual trip home.

Many of the leading brands in our industry, including Mandarin Oriental, Peninsula, Rosewood and Shangri -La are Hong Kong based. The Hong Kong government has also designated human capital in travel and hospitality as a high priority for its investment program matching ventures with industry corporates and investors in Greater China.

在中国建立业务的美国传统品牌正面临巨大挑战。在未来几年中，本土新贵将会出现，并将受到中国消费者的青睐。那些将中国市场视为创新之源的老牌企业，将继续生存。新一代的行业领袖要能够抓住机遇，在中国建立有利可图的国内业务。

于这些原因，我于2019年创立的Mogul Hospitality 公司正在进入中国市场。 我们的使命是通过不断创新的酒店管理体系，为中国酒店业的员工提供更大的发展空间。 我们还把当地社区的行动重点，放在表彰外来的3千万务工人员，其中大多数已为人母，她们占中国酒店劳动力市场的近三分之一，她们与家人分开生活，每年只有一次返乡探亲的机会。

我们行业中的许多国际知名品牌，包括文华东方酒店、半岛酒店、瑰丽酒店和香格里拉酒店，都位于香港。 香港政府还将旅游业和酒店业的人力资本，作为其投资计划的重中之重，以便与大中华地区的企业和投资者建立合资企业。

The massive government stimulus after the pandemic and the turmoil in its real estate market also represents a once in a generation opportunity for the most innovative U.S. based brands to ramp up investing in China and targeting its domestic market. We are also seeing this happen with many recent entrants such as Tesla and Disney theme parks. These cross- cultural brands in essential industries such as electric vehicles and education, have brilliant timing. As part of its post Covid-19 stimulus plan, China will be investing trillions of RMB into EV, Biotech and service sectors. The ramped-up spending will aim to spur infrastructure investment, backed by as much as 2.8 trillion yuan ($394 billion) of local government special bonds.

疫情过后，政府的大规模刺激措施以及房地产市场的动荡，也为美国最具创新精神的品牌，提供了一个千载难逢的机会，这些品牌可以加大在中国的投资力度，瞄准中国的国内市场。特斯拉（Tesla）和1 Hotels等许多新玩家身上，我们就看到了这一点。这些跨文化品牌，在支柱产业中有着绝佳时机。作为疫情过后经济刺激计划的一部分，中国政府将向服务业、电动汽车、生物技术行业投资数万亿元人民币。增加支出的目的是刺激基础设施投资，由高达2.8万亿元人民币（合3940亿美元）的地方政府的专项作为支持。

For example, Tesla recently took 10,000 orders after building a $5B factory in China with a new global R&D center.

特斯拉（Tesla）最近接到了1万份订单，此前该公司在中国投资50亿美元，建立了一家工厂，并设立了一个新的全球研发中心。

How should you approach the market and what does it take to succeed in China? Having helped many brands enter the market and been the CEO of a Chinese based company that created a new category, I will share my top 8 (lucky) lessons.

如果您有看透政治的能力，并考虑在全球范围内推广自己的品牌，则应考虑在未来12个月，利用中国即将到来的经济复苏的机会。您应该如何打入中国市场，如何在中国取得成功？在帮助了许多品牌进入中国市场，并担任过一家创建新类别的中国公司的CEO之后，我将分享我的八大经验（幸运数字8）.

1. **Build a Purpose Driven Brand/Zhenchendge/Wang Ming**
   建立目标驱动的品牌/真诚的/Wang Ming

If your brand passes the Chinese measure of sincerity, or "Zhenchendge," and makes a positive social impact and you're in it for the long term, consider expanding into China.

如果您的品牌通过了中国的诚信标准，即"真诚的"，并且对社会产生了积极的影响，并且长期处于这种影响力中，那么考虑将业务扩展到中国。

Chinese consumers have become more sophisticated, more worldly and more socially conscious. President Xi's anti-corruption and anti-consumption campaign has been successful and conspicuous consumption is out of favor. Chinese consumers, led by Millennials and Gen X/Gen Y, are seeking individualized experiences with authentic brands with a purpose and social cause.

中国消费者变得越来越成熟，更加多层次，越来越具有社会意识。习近平主席的"反腐倡廉"运动取得了成功，炫耀性消费失宠。以千禧一代（Millennials）和X/Y一代（Gen X/Gen Y）为首的中国消费者，正在寻求具有目的性和社会性的纯正品牌的个性化体验。

Consider a key finding of Peking University Professor Lisa Grunberg's ethnographic research of the K11 mall in Shanghai:

以北京大学教授丽莎·格伦伯格（Lisa Grunberg）对上海K11购物中心的"民族志研究"为例

"This growing sense of regard for local brands comes despite years of mistrust in local producers, as a general sense of national pride is increasing alongside local quality standards. In many cases, China's local brands are much more able to tap into local stories and narratives. Considering that the geopolitical tensions and even the recent coronavirus outbreak are further fueling this sense of national pride, it is likely that as well as catering to exciting and unique offline experiences, appealing to this new identity will be increasingly important.

"尽管多年来人们一直不信任本地生产商，但人们对本土品牌的这种日益增长的尊重之情依然存在，因为随着当地质量标准的提高，人们普遍的民族自豪感也在增强。在很多情况下，中国本土品牌更有能力挖掘本土故事和事件。考虑到地缘政治的紧张局势，甚至是最近的冠状病毒爆发，都在进一步加剧这种民族自豪感，因此，品牌除了提供创新和独特的线下体验外，利用这种民族自豪感的新身份，也将变得越来越重要。"

In response to changes in Chinese consumer preferences and government policies, the market entry and development strategy adopted by these affordable, socially conscious brands such as Tesla and Disney is a throwback to the days before corporate globalization as we know it. They have adopted what Harvard Business School Professor Michael Yoshino calls a "multi-domestic strategy," where China is treated as a distinct local market with local production and operations.

为了响应中国消费者偏好和政府政策的变化，这些价格实惠、具有社会意识的品牌所采取的市场进入和发展战略，是一种倒退，回到了我们所知的企业全球化之前的时代。这些品牌采取了哈佛商学院（Harvard Business School）教授吉野幸男（Michael Yoshino）所称的"多国本土化战略"（multi-domestic strategy），即中国被视为一个独特的本地市场，拥有本地生产和运营。

To grow a brand in China today, business leaders must develop a clear plan and message for how it will improve the quality of life for Chinese citizens. Consider the case study of Tesla. Tesla invested $5 billion into its Chinese factory to sell cars in the country and Tencent is one of its biggest shareholders. No foreign company has invested in a bigger Chinese factory than Tesla, which aims to have 100% of parts locally sourced by the end of 2020. Tesla is developing a Chinese design and engineering center to develop new cars specifically for the China market. Their approach to the China market has resulted in various concessions including tax credits, subsidies, faster approvals and preferential loans. Prices for Tesla's Model 3 sedans are similar to local manufacturers such as NIO Inc. and Xpeng Motors, while undercutting global players such as BMW and Daimler AG.

要在今天的中国发展一个品牌，商业领袖必须制定一个清晰的计划和传达一个明确的信息，说明企业会如何改善中国公民的生活质量。以特斯拉（Tesla）为例。特斯拉（Tesla）向其中国工厂投资50亿美元，以在中国销售汽车，腾讯是其最大的股东之一。没有一家外国公司在中国投资的工厂比特斯拉（Tesla）的更大。特斯拉（Tesla）的目标是，到2020年底，所有零部件都在中国本土采购。特斯拉（Tesla）正在建立一个中国设计和工程中心，专门为中国市场开发新车。特斯拉（Tesla）这种进入中国市场的模式，获得了各种优惠，包括税收抵免、补贴、快速审批和优惠贷款。特斯拉Model 3轿车的价格，与本地制造商如蔚来汽车（NIO Inc. ）和小鹏汽车（Xpeng Motors）的价格相近，削弱了宝马（BMW）和戴姆勒（Daimler AG）等全球汽车制造商的竞争力。

Similarly, many American legacy brands have also found a 2nd life in China due to deep local partnerships, including General Motors (Buick is the #1 selling vehicle) and Howard Johnson (which, almost extinct in the U.S., has over 100 five-star hotels in China). This has happened in large part because the local partners have made a positive social impact with local and provincial governments, and are effectively their equity investors and lenders. In almost all cases, business leaders must maintain strong relationships with government officials who are measured on job and wealth creation and social capital. Having transformed their country, most Chinese business leaders are now motivated by "Wang ming" or a higher level of "total dedication." Offering a brand or business that becomes a new global standard and improves the environment or has a positive social impact scores highest.

由于与当地伙伴的深度合作，许多美国传统品牌在中国找到了第二人生，包括通用汽车（别克是销量排名第一的汽车）和豪生酒店（Howard Johnson® 在美国几乎消失，但在中国拥有100多家五星级酒店）。 之所以出现这种情况，很大程度上是因为当地的合作伙伴，对地方政府和省级政府，产生了积极的社会影响，实际上他们也是股权投资者和贷款人。几乎在所有情况下，企业领导者都必须与政府官员保持密切的关系，而政府官员对企业的衡量标准，是这些企业为当地创造了多少就业，带来了多少财富和社会资本。在中国产业升级之后，现在大多数中国企业领导人的动力来自Wang Ming（"皇命"？），或者更高层次的"全心全意为人民服务"。如果品牌或企业，提供新的全球标准、改善环境或具有积极的社会影响力，这样的品牌或企业，进入中国市场获得成功的机会最大。

2. **Many businesses and brands seek to enter the China market with a deal or project and set up an office in Hong Kong. This is the wrong mindset. Rather than executing a transaction, aspiring global brands are better off setting up a listening post in mainland China to study and explore the market.**

发现中国/学习中国文化

许多企业和品牌，都希望通过一次交易或一个项目，进入中国市场，并在香港设立办事处。这是错误的心态。与其只是完成一桩交易，品牌们最好在中国大陆设立据点，来研究和探索中国市场。

The era when you could simply do a single transaction and enter the Chinese market with a foreign brand is coming to an end. The hotel industry is a case in point. According to C-Trip and the Chinese Tourism Authority, China's domestic tourism spend is over $700 billion, almost 7 times its often lauded $115 billion outbound travel spend. In the coming years, Chinese hotel owners may decide to phase out international brands and begin to manage their own properties. For example, the Wanda Group, which currently owns hotels managed by IHG, Hyatt, and Hilton, in addition to Accor, is allowing existing contracts with foreign partners to expire, according to the Nikkei report, and will opt to self-manage any new hotels it develops under its own operating company. Capital Tourism Group, the listed arm of Beijing Tourism, China's largest state-owned tourism conglomerate, is also setting up its own chain of luxury hotels.

简单地与外国品牌达成交易，然后该品牌顺利进入中国市场的时代即将结束。酒店业就是一个很好的例子。根据携程网和中国旅游局的数据，中国国内旅游支出，超过7,000亿美元，几乎是其经常称赞的1,150亿美元出境旅游支出的7倍。在这种背景下，中国的酒店业主正在逐步淘汰国际品牌，开始管理自己的酒店。根据《日本经济新闻》（Nikkei）的报道，目前，万达目前拥有由洲际酒店集团（IHG）、凯悦集团（Hyatt）、希尔顿集团（Hilton），以及雅高集团（Accor）管理的酒店，万达将终止与这些外国合作伙伴的现有合同，并选择自行管理其在自己的运营公司下开发的新酒店。首都旅游集团（Capital Tourism Group）是中国最大的国有旅游企业集团北京旅游（Beijing Tourism）的上市子公司，目前正在建立自己的豪华连锁酒店。

1 Hotels, a highly differentiated, sustainable hotel brand developed by U.S. industry pioneer Barry Sternlicht of Starwood Capital is slated to open its first eco-boutique resort in Sanya, China. As a truly sustainable brand made from local materials at the highest environmental standards, this "Tesla of hotels," is a relevant brand entering China at the right time. Eco-boutique and sustainable hotel brands such as Aman, Banyan Tree and URBN by Cachet hotels may experience significant demands in China in the near future.

由美国酒店业先驱，有"喜达屋之父"之称的Barry Sternlicht开发的高度差异化、可持续发展的酒店品牌1 Hotels，计划在中国三亚，开设首家生态精品酒店度假村。以最高的环保标准使用当地材料，打造一个真正可持续发展的品牌，这个酒店界的"特斯拉"，是在对的时间进入中国市场的品牌之一。

China is a 5000-year-old civilization but a relatively young country founded in 1949. Like most large countries, mainland China is very regional, diverse and multicultural. For centuries it was fragmented into fiefdoms, each run by its own warlord. Chinese people embrace foreigners who study their dynastic history, ethnic groups and language. A deep understanding of the ten languages and dialects, including Mandarin (Putonghua), Cantonese (Yue), Shanghainese (Wu) and others is just the beginning. Foreign business leaders should familiarize themselves with Chinese classic literature starting with the Tang Dynasty (618-097 A.D.) which included Tzu, Confucius and Mencius.

中国是一个有着5000年历史的文明古国，但却又是一个相对年轻的国家，于1949年成立。与大多数大国一样，中国大陆地域辽阔，文化多样。几个世纪以来，中国被分割成多个领地，每个领地都由自己的军阀统治。中国人欢迎外国人学习中国的王朝历史、传统文化和民族语言。深入了解十种语言和方言，包括普通话、广东话（粤语）、上海话（吴语）等，仅仅是一个开始。外国商界领袖应该熟悉从唐朝（公元618-097年）开始的中国古典文学，包括有关老子、孔子和孟子的文化。

Impatient deal-makers or "Cowboys" with short attention spans are ill-suited to doing business in China. Any business leader who seeks to build a successful venture in China must possess an intellectual curiosity and passion for learning. A Chinese market leader must have a unique ability to understand patterns of thought and behavior or "Wenhua," reflected in Chinese culture. This is imperative to understand the internal contradictions between authoritarian style communism and ruthless capitalism. It is imperative to travel across the regions, from Jiangsu to Fujian and Sichuan province and to 2nd and 3rd tier cities where most of the economic development is now occurring. Across regions, there is a wide diversity of work cultures and government roles in financing companies and approving projects and local business leaders. Each region has its own "weltanschauung" (German word for worldview) and international trading and investment relationships.

任何想在中国成功创业的商界领袖，都必须具备求知欲和学习热情。中国市场的领导者，必须有一种独特的能力，去理解中国文化中所反映的思维模式和行为模式，或所谓的中国"文化"。这对于理解独裁式共产主义和残酷资本主义之间的内在矛盾，至关重要。省际旅行非常有必要，从江苏省到福建省、四川省，再到目前经济发展最快的二、三线城市。在各个地区，对于企业融资、审批项目和当地商业领袖等方面，存在着广泛的工作文化和政府角色的多样性。每个地区都有自己的世界观，以及国际贸易和投资关系。

3. Build Deep Partnerships/Jiao Pengyou (T'su-oh Pung-yoh-ou)

建立深厚的伙伴关系/交朋友

In China, the expression "Jiao Pengyou" ("to make friends") is absolutely critical. Friendships, or Youyi, are everything. Typically, it's necessary to get introductions from third parties who are in favor and well acquainted with individuals you want to do business with, often through personal family contacts. This is different than the basis for business relationships in the West. It's less about those similar interests, and hard facts and more about emotional intelligence. Youyi is typically facilitated by 3rd parties and is established in person through social engagements.

（展示2016年开业的昆明彩云里•凯世精品酒店签约仪式的图片）
在中国，"交朋友"很重要。友谊就是一切。通常情况下，如果您想和某人做生意，你必须从熟悉这个某人的第三方那里，获得牵线搭桥，得到引荐，通常这个第三方是通过私人的家庭联系，来为您做介绍。这与西方建立关系的基础不同。在中国建立关系，人们更少关注相似的兴趣爱好和硬性事实，而更多关注情商。友谊通常由第三方推动，并通过社交活动亲自建立。

This is not to suggest that Chinese business leaders and state-owned enterprises are not intellectual or driven by knowledge, or "Shi," evidenced by the culture of nation-wide testing, including in philosophy. The Chinese can be aggressive dealmakers and have extraordinary respect for knowledge and experience. But Americans seeking to establish their business in China should shift their mindset away from cold data and hard facts that support a business case. If you approach a relationship with a client, partner, vendor or employee as a deal or a business case subject to western style universal ethics, you are not likely to succeed.

这并不是说中国的商界领袖、国有企业领导者不是知识分子，不是由知识驱动，或者不是"士"，全国范围内的考试文化（包括哲学）就证明了这一点。中国人非常尊重知识。但是，寻求在中国建立业务的美国人，应该改变其思维方式，远离那些支持商业案例的冰冷数据和确凿事实。如果您处理与客户、合作伙伴、供应商或员工之间的关系，就像处理一笔交易或一个商业案例一样，遵循西方普遍的道德规范，那么就不太可能成功。

4. Manage the Lawyers and Keep Deals High Level

管理律师，保持高水平交易

Confucius believed that people play by the rules because of their inherent virtue, rather than man-made laws or "falv." Even today, Beijing prefers to issue directives rather than write laws. Lawyers don't play a significant role in Chinese business transactions or in managing conflicts especially once you're in business. In my experience, lawyers typically show up at the end of a deal and do what they are told. Due diligence on new friends is not performed by accountants and lawyers, and business contracts may have little to do with how business may evolve in the future.

孔子认为，人们遵守规则是因为其内在美德，而不是人为的法律或"法"，即使在今天，中国政府也更倾向于发布指令，而不是制定法律。在中国开展业务后，律师在中国的商业交易或处理纠纷中，不会发挥重要作用。律师通常会在交易结束时出现，并按要求行事。对"新朋友"的尽职调查，并不是由会计师和律师进行的，商业合同可能与未来的业务发展没有多大关系。

5. Budget Five Times Longer than Anticipated and Keep Negotiating/Tan Pan

预估时间比预期多五倍，并持续谈判

Building relationships requires considerable time and money investment anywhere in the world. But in China, it requires numerous events, dinners, social functions and numerous trips. If you're in a hurry, it will be obvious, and the other side will either take advantage or just quickly extract intellectual property from you and declare victory. The Chinese also like to negotiate or "Tan Pan," even after the deal is signed. If you budgeted 2 months, assume it will take 10 months. Often, the deal never ends, so appoint a relationship manager who has deal fluency and is bilingual. Regardless of where and how disputes may be settled, the Chinese version of the agreement is all that matters. And don't be surprised if at the last minute you receive a message requesting more changes including a phone call or knock on your door right before a signing ceremony from a legal representative or translator acting on their own behalf to renegotiate. That has happened to me a few times (unbeknownst to the chairperson) and in retrospect it probably means I scored some points in the negotiation.

在世界任何地方建立关系，都需要投入大量的时间和金钱。但在中国，这需要无数的活动、晚宴、社交活动和无数次差旅。如果您很着急达成交易，那就很明显了，对方要么会占便宜，要么就迅速从您那里获取信息，然后宣布胜利。中国人喜欢谈判，甚至在协议签署之后也是如此。如果您预计要花2个月进行谈判，那就假设需要10个月。交易永无止境，因此请任命一位具有专业知识，且会说双语的客户经理。无论争端在和储备如何解决，这份协议的中文版本才是最重要的。如果在签字仪式开始前的最后一分钟，对方的代表律师或翻译，给您发信息、打电话，甚至是敲您的门，要求重新谈判，进行更多更改，也请不要感到惊讶。这种情况在我身上发生过几次，现在回想起来，这可能意味着我在谈判中获得了一些优势。

6. Keep a Close Eye on People but Practice Mianzi/Avoid Choh-ou

密切注意周围的人，给面子/避免让人当众出丑

Westerners believe in 360-degree feedback and are used to a "thick skinned" work environment where employees, business contacts and government officials can be openly critiqued. In contrast, the Chinese believe in Confucian-based harmony. "Chou" or smelly criticism on an individual level, can be dangerous and when necessary should be done privately and diplomatically. Criticism of government or public officials is considered treason.

西方人相信360度的反馈，习惯于"厚脸皮"的工作环境。在这种环境中，员工、业务联系人和政府官员，都可以受到公开批评。相比之下，中国人相信以儒家思想为基础的"和谐"，让人"当众出丑"或个人层面的严厉批评，是不合时宜的，必要时应该私下圆融地进行交涉。对政府或公职人员的公开批评被视为叛国罪。

The Chinese concept of "face" or Mianzi means respecting and complimenting others so they give you face in return. One of the common issues facing foreign business leaders in China is how to address western definitions of conflicts of interest or corruption. In China, locals are often on both or multiple sides of a deal. It is considered acceptable in business, especially if the parties are contractors or brokers. Certain foreign countries acknowledge this and their legal segments enable their companies to make "investments" that are illegal for U.S. companies. While the contractors and locals are under Chinese law and it's hard to be sure who is doing what, make sure it's clear where you stand but communicate it privately and diplomatically.

中国人所说的给"面子"是指尊重和称赞他人，这样他们也会给您"面子"。外国企业领导人在中国面临的一个共同问题是，在西方看来存在利益冲突或腐败时，在中国如何处理？在中国，当地人往往是一笔交易的一方或多方。这在商业上被认可，是可以接受的，特别是当事人

是承包商或中间人时。某些国家允许其公司进行一些对美国公司来说是非法的投资。虽然承包商和当地人都受中国法律的约束，但我们也不清楚他们的角色划分，请确保您的立场明确，必要时要私下用圆融的手段进行沟通。

7. Enable "Can do" Chinese Partners to Innovate/Ganjin

使"能干"的中国合作伙伴能够创新/有干劲

There is considerable innovation in China and in many industries and disciplines such as biotech, EV and artificial intelligence, China is setting new global standards for quality in a number of industries, led by the Ganjin, or new generation of entrepreneurs that number in the millions who have the ambition, courage and strength to take risks.

American business leaders must protect their brands and intellectual properties but the larger opportunity is to use China as a fertile ground to create new products. Hence, it's best to keep standards and requirements at a high level and approach the Chinese as a partner in innovation and brand -building, not as a market to harvest a brand.

中国的许多行业都有相当大的创新，如生物技术、电动汽车和人工智能，中国正在设立新的全球质量标准，由数以百万计的有雄心、有勇气、有实力去冒险的新一代企业家领导。

归根结底，美国商业领袖必须保护自己的品牌和知识产权，但不能像在美国国内那样。最好是保持较高的标准和要求，把中国作为品牌创新和品牌建设的合作伙伴，而不是一个收获口碑的市场。

8. Be Discreet/Zhongguo

谨行慎言/中国化

The N.B.A. has targeted China for roughly a half-century, investing $10 billion into the market to build a fan base among 1.4 billion people. China now has more fans of the league than there are in the United States, a country of 330 million. Before the pandemic, the N.B.A.'s top stars routinely traveled to the country between seasons to promote sneakers. Since 2004, the N.B.A. has played dozens of games there. In 2019, the National Basketball Association (NBA), got into trouble after Houston Rockets General Manager Daryl Morey tweeted — and quickly deleted — a message of support for Hong Kong, NBA Commissioner Adam Silver issued contradictory statements defending the NBA's stance to Americans and apologizing to the Chinese. With the blockage of NBA games from CCTV and Tencent this season, the most ardent Chinese observers have searched out "illegal channels," such as pirated live streams offered by some sports booking services. When Tencent's services were available, few bothered to watch the illegal content, which usually is of poorer quality. The fan demand is undeniable, three years later, the NBA players returned to state-run television in China. Getting canceled for 3 years cost the NBA an estimated $400 million dollars. But there's a bigger lesson here for American companies about how to do business in China.

N.B.A.已经将中国作为目标大约半个世纪, 投资了100亿美元进入中国市场, 以在14亿人口中建立球迷基础。中国现在拥有的N.B.A.球迷比美国还多, 美国有3.3亿人口。在大流行病爆发之前, N.B.A.的顶级球星通常会在赛季之间前往中国宣传球鞋。自2004年以来, N.B.A.在中国举办了数十场比赛。2019年, 休斯顿火箭队总经理莫里 (Daryl Morey) 在推特上发了一条 (随后迅速删除) 支持香港抗争者的推文后, NBA陷入困境, NBA总裁亚当·西尔弗 (Adam Silver) 发表了自相矛盾的声明, 向美国人捍卫NBA的立场, 并向中国人道歉。随着本赛季央视和腾讯平台对NBA比赛的封锁, 热心的中国球迷纷纷搜索 "非法频道", 例如一些体育博彩服务提供的盗版直播。腾讯平台提供该节目时, 很少有人愿意观看这些通常质量较差的非官方内容。球迷的需求是不可否认的, 一旦NBA恢复比赛, NBA将会回到中国。但是, 对于在中国开展业务的美国品牌来说, 这是一个重要的教训。

In China, social change is a long and gradual process that is best handled privately and behind doors. A single, impulsive tweet from the equivalent of a brand leader resulted in a 3 year ban and billions of dollars of damage to the NBA and its Chinese partners Tencent and CCTV.

在中国，社会变革是一个漫长而循序渐进的过程，最好是私下或者通过"后门"来应对。一条来自品牌领导者的冲动性推文，对NBA及其中国合作伙伴腾讯（Tencent）和央视（CCTV），造成了数十亿美元的损失。

Furthermore, discretion is a form of social capital built by powerful government officials and business leaders who led by example. If you intend to build a brand or business in China, practice Confucian principles and blend in with the people. Make sure your car is the latest bestselling Buick minivan. If you fly private, don't talk about it. If you're a foreigner, carry a Chinese phone so your local employees can communicate with you on WeChat.

此外，谨慎也需要以身作则。如果打算在中国建立品牌或业务，请遵循儒家思想，融入中国人民。确保您的座驾是最畅销的别克商务车，如果您乘坐私人飞机，请避免提及。如果您是一个外国人，请您携带一部中国品牌的手机，这样本地员工可以使用微信与您沟通。

I worked with many China based billionaires and princelings who dressed simply, dined in private dining rooms of public restaurants, and did not travel with an entourage.

我曾与中国的许多亿万富翁和官二代共事，他们衣着简朴，没有随行人员陪同。

● Conclusion: Calling All Disruptors - China is Back

结论：对所有颠覆者喊话——中国又回来了

The old expression "China is the factory of the world," is outdated. Most of China's current and future GDP is services and driven by technology innovation. In contrast to India, even before the U.S. immigration bottleneck, a new generation of leaders educated at top U.S., Canadian, UK and Australian universities was coming back to

China. Consequently, China has established leadership positions in many high-tech sectors including health care, biotech, social media, online education, human resources technologies, telecommunications, entertainment, and travel.

"中国是世界工厂"这句老话已经过时。 中国GDP的绝大一部分是由服务业，以及科技创新所驱动。 与印度相反，即使在美国移民限制之前，在美国顶尖大学中受过教育的新一代中国领导人正在回到中国。 因此，中国在医疗保健、生物科技、社交媒体、在线教育、人力资源技术、电信、娱乐和旅游等许多高科技领域，都处于领先地位。

Similar to the post-2008 financial crisis, Beijing is aggressively investing in rebuilding the ailing Chinese economy. The marriage between the U.S. and China is over and the process of decoupling has commenced, which may disrupt incumbent category leaders. The economic opportunity in China is bigger than ever and a new wave of innovation is coming quickly to serve a more sophisticated consumer who looks beyond social status and towards purpose driven brands that make a positive impact China and the world.

与2008年金融危机过后的做法类似，中国政府正在大举投资重建中国经济。中美两国的联姻已经结束，脱钩进程已经开始，这将对现有的行业领导者产生负面影响。中国的经济机遇比以往任何时候都更大，新一轮的创新浪潮正在迅速到来，以服务于更为成熟的中国消费者，这将超越社会地位，转向对中国和世界产生积极影响的目标驱动品牌。

"I'm increasingly inclined to think that there should be some regulatory oversight, maybe at the national and international level, just to make sure that we don't do something very foolish. I mean with artificial intelligence we're summoning the demon."

Elon Musk

EPILOGUE
A CALL TO ACTION: RESPONSIBLE AI

In November 2023, the long-simmering fault-lines in the debate over AI safety reached a new crescendo with the non-profit board of OpenAI, the creator of ChatGPT and DALL-E services, voting to fire its founder & CEO Sam Altman. Within the U.S. technology community, two opposing factions have emerged: the "doomers" or self-described "safety-first technocrats" led by venture firms such as General Catalyst (in partnership with the Biden Administration) who are forming cross-disciplinary committees and non-profits that create protocols and playbooks; and the "humanists," also known as the "techno-optimists" led by libertarian firms like Andreesen Horowitz who believe entrepreneurs rather than policymakers (who are seeking to relitigate regulation more broadly) or non-profits who have never built things are most capable of ensuring technology is a force for good. The debate risks tearing Silicon Valley apart and given the heightened risks for investors, negatively impacting U.S. leadership, with unintended consequences such as AI offshoring that may benefit regions such as the E.U, that have established regulatory frameworks, countries such as China where businesses are engaged in multi-year state-sponsored AI initiatives.

Over the past few years, the "doomers" or safety-first technocrats have been gathering momentum. There have been considerable multilateral efforts to establish an agreed upon terminology, development guardrails, auditing standards and compliance systems for the responsible development and release of generative artificial intelligence. Policymakers around the world, including the EU, U.S., UK, Canada, Japan, and Australia were frantically enacting new AI regulations. The EU's proposed AI Act seeks to heavily regulate a group of systems that threaten human rights and safety including automated hiring and real time biometric surveillance. These precipitous developments raise an important strategic question for executives in hospitality and travel: should they regulate AI and if so - when, how, and where?

• Defining The Problem

Artificial intelligence (AI) can be defined simply as "the capability of a machine to imitate intelligent human behavior." The OECD defines AI as "a machine-based system that can, for a given set of human defined-objectives, make predictions, recommendations or decisions influencing real or virtual environments." It classifies AI cases into one of the following 6 types: hyper-personalization, recognition, conversation and human interaction, predictive decision and analytics, goal-driven systems, autonomous systems and patterns and anomalies.

Moderna used AI and robotic automation to produce 1,000 mRNAs a month, a molecule that was essential to the vaccine's development and production scale. The health care industry is investing billions of dollars in AI to advance precision health and responsible health care intelligence. Examples of use cases in precision health include apps that analyze dietary habits and provide reports on the nutritional intake of each menu on personal mobile devices starting with senior care facilities and children with chronic diseases. With respect to health care intelligence, AI algorithms are analyzing medical imaging data to identify early signs of disease, with far greater accuracy than human doctors and at a lower cost. By combining these innovations with the power of genomics, machine learning and AI will transform the healthcare industry and eliminate its labor shortages in the coming years.

The travel industry has been experimenting with AI, automation, and robotics for at least a decade including automated lighting, automated vehicles, and biometric identification. In China, Alibaba has been working with international hotel chains on full-service robot hotels that check customers using biometrics, deliver room supplies and meals in restaurants and even act as bartenders. In the U.S., an M.I.T. backed restaurant chain called Spyce created the first robotic restaurant that delivers meals in less than three minutes priced 40% less than comparable quick service brands; its technologies have been adopted by Sweetgreen, a fast-growing brand that claims to be "all in on automation." Online travel agencies such as booking.com are introducing AI trip planners that predict travel intent and create visual lists of destinations and properties. The goal of these companies and a wave of new travel AI start-ups is to establish automated systems that don't just imitate human intelligence, but far surpass it in terms of the scale of data, learning and predictions required to personalize the customer experience.

Source: *Artificial Intelligence & Responsible Business Conduct* report, OECD

● A Renewed Sense of Urgency

After decades of investments, trillion-dollar big tech companies such as Microsoft (Open AI/Chat GPT) and Google (Bard) gave premature birth to AI in the public domain. They claimed their primary motivation was to carefully test generative AI on a large scale with real users to garner feedback akin to what start-ups do when they launch an imperfect minimum viable product (MVP) ripe with flaws and defects. However, skeptics contend they accelerated its launch to defend their turf in businesses such as search engines and to raise large amounts of capital at high valuations to pre-empt their rivals. Observers noted their timing was no coincidence: it capitalized on rising anti-China sentiments among polarized Western governments who were not capable of bipartisan legislation.

Few in Washington D.C., Ottawa or Brussels were surprised that the CEOs of these big technology firms advocated AI regulations, such as open innovation and levels of transparency they failed themselves to provide the public. The paradox is that these Western technology firms, who have become far more powerful than national governments with respect to their wealth and scale, are the only ones capable of leading the process to establish Responsible AI.

● The Promise of Multilateralism 2.0

Global AI regulatory efforts are rooted in a philosophy of multilateralism that Princeton scholar Robert Keohane characterized as "a persistent and connected set of rules, [that] prescribe behavioral roles, constrain activity and shape expectations," thus affecting the behavior of all actors. In the early 1990s, after the collapse of the Berlin War, Keohane defined "the new multilateralism" as "the practice of coordinating national policies in groups of three or more states, through ad-hoc arrangements or by means of institutions." When multilateralism works, nations and civilizations recognize their fates are indivisibly linked, and their interactions are based on generalized principles of conduct and expectations of diffuse reciprocity. Since 2021, ad-hoc multilateral efforts at advancing Responsible AI – multilateralism 2.0 - have been quite inclusive, involving big tech, start-ups, government representatives, academics, non-governmental organizations, and members of civil society. The objective is to establish adaptive and interoperable AI regulatory frameworks and harmonized standards such as those being developed by the U.S. National Institute of Standards and Technology (NIST), requiring "red teaming" as a testing system.

Perhaps most notably, international organizations such as the World Economic Forum's AI Governance Alliance (which published recommendations on precise and shared terminology, model and system traceability and knowledge sharing that prioritizes social progress) and the OECD (whose comprehensive framework addresses data relevance and representativeness, data quality, understanding systems decisions, transparency to the user and data subject, bias testing and robust systems testing) organized summits featuring a diverse cross-section of experts that appeared aligned with new standards and protocols for AI engineering. In 2022, the Responsible AI Institute (RAII) created a global certification program that has been adopted by certain industries such as financial services who have implemented its programs in automated lending. G7 leaders have also agreed on International Guiding Principles on AI

In the U.S., President Biden released his Executive Order on Safe, Secure and Trustworthy AI which followed the U.S. Commerce departments AI Risk Management Framework which took a sectoral approach in negotiation with major AI companies. Critics have remarked that these efforts are little more than vaporware. Unlike the E.U's AI Act, which calls for testing and documentation, these initiatives lack teeth and will require legislation and are subject to judicial review and can be revoked by a future administration.

● The Limits of AI Sovereignty

Given the stakes for national security in an unstable multi-polar world, governments are not betting on multilateralism 2.0. Hence, the race is on and AI sovereignty reigns supreme. As a case in point, Germany's research minister Bettina Stark-Watzinger framed the new EU AI Action Plan as a way to achieve "technological sovereignty" and avoid dependence on outside powers. This came weeks after Germany announced its own multi-billion-dollar AI fund citing "AI sovereignty" in a global competition against the U.S. and China as Berlins' top priority.

At recent AI summit in London that included Chinese representatives, UK Prime Minister Rishi Sunak, a Stanford MBA who has financed many technology start-ups in his career, argued that "only governments can properly assess the risks to national security" and that "only nation states have the power and legitimacy to keep their people safe." The problem is that people have historically low levels of confidence in their government leaders, irrespective of whether they are democracies or not. It's also difficult for citizens to place their faith in many of the same politicians who failed to enact meaningful regulations on internet search or social media. They failed to ban data brokerages that sell users data to organizations based anywhere in the world. Furthermore, some of the proposed regulations – like requiring AI to know why the system does what it does in each case - are not just utopian, they demonstrate that most legislators fail to grasp even the basic concepts of AI.

Geopolitics is throwing more fuel on the fire. While some Western politicians believe it's best to leave Beijing out of the process altogether, the irony is that China is the only major G20 country that has enacted regulations addressing hate speech on social media, curtailing children's time playing video games and regulating surveillance technologies and facial recognition. As Elon Musk points out, how could a global governance model possibly exclude China?

The paradox of Responsible AI is that the superpowers today are not governments – they are big technology firms. Multilateralism 2.0 is appropriately described by Ian Bremmer as a new "techno-polar world order." The more viable resolution is self-regulation with Elon Musk, Satya Nadella, or Jensen Huang playing the role of Captain Kirk in the U.S. Enterprise, chairing AI governance, resolving disputes and dispatching multinational inspection teams that put out fires and advise governments how to manage risks.

● Recommendations for the Hospitality and Travel Industry

Chaos is not an option for travel and hospitality, an industry that thrives on stability. The unprecedented "techno-polar" context should not dissuade CEOs in the travel and hospitality industry from establishing a process for collective AI security. Regrettably, the hospitality industry is widely regarded as a sleeper with respect to cybersecurity as evidenced by the recent attacks that paralyzed MGM resorts and resulted in Caesars Entertainment paying multi-million-dollar ransoms to hackers. Over the past decade, most of the world's largest hotel chains, including Hyatt and Marriott, have been hacked several times, resulting in the travel records and credit card information of over 40 million people being exposed and huge fines from governments such as the UK. Compounding the situation is the fact that hospitality and travel firms generally outsource their software development, security, and technology infrastructure to consulting firms who rely on a network of offshore vendors. Most travel and hospitality firms and their franchisees lack the expertise to audit AI engineering in house and are not trained in writing large language models.

Given these realities, the industry should move quickly to establish a process to regulate AI, prioritizing the following three initiatives: (1) Creating a single multilateral organization for responsible AI in travel and hospitality including an auditing and certification process managed by an independent third party; (2) Adopting new corporate governance standards that mandate AI literacy for all employees and board directors that sit on an AI committee of the board; and (3) Prioritize multilateral projects that establish new standards and protocols for the use of artificial intelligence in human capital management.

Responsible AI requires establishing global auditing standards and requirements, starting with authenticating AI-generated content, user testing and content traceability in areas that protect consumers including privacy. For example, as travel planning, hotel bookings and check-in get automated, there are serious risks not just to privacy but security. If terrorists hack into a hotel reservation system and direct a target into a specific hotel room or vacation rental home and subsequently take over the cameras and launch an attack, it would have devastating consequences for the entire travel industry. Encrypting personal information, including names and contact information, could be a first step towards privacy and security.

Travelers need to know when AI is used and how it's employed as well as how and where to provide timely feedback and complaints. Other issues to explore include synthetic data and media which can speed up developments such as customer value scoring for the purpose of determining a reward program tier but are likely to exacerbate bias or even create new biases. Hotel and airline websites should publish a Model Card for each new version of an A.I. model that is deployed including how the model is used, as well as information on safety evaluations conducted to test the model.

To diversify the supply base, hotels and airlines must work together to establish an open-source innovation platform that shares best practices and is overseen by independent experts. To foster trust with consumers, travel and hospitality companies should require their teams and vendors develop "secure by design software" rather than endless patches to fix software vulnerabilities that are commonplace today. It's imperative that new travel AI standards and protocols don't perpetuate the dominance or control of AI development by either big technology firms or the handful of incumbent technology players who presently dominate the supply base of vendors in platforms such as online distribution, reservations, revenue, and channel management, as well as human resources technologies.

Regulations are long overdue to address AI's growing role in human capital. At present, few AI-powered tools for recruitment and selection are fully explainable and interpretable or can prove they do not disadvantage a minority group. The scope should include auditing all recruitment-related software starting with applicant tracking systems and job sites for systematic bias. The truth is that the process was deeply flawed prior to the advent of AI, filtering out semi qualified workers, most notably women, minorities and military veterans and exacerbating historic labor shortages. Upgrading human resource departments in travel and hospitality to become sufficiently technology literate should be the highest training priority. New regulations should force HR software firms to be transparent about their data practices and provide operators the ability to use artificial intelligence to engineer their own talent marketplaces and reduce their dependence on third party human capital software intermediaries.

It's time for executives in the travel and hospitality industry – which accounts for 300 million global employees that represent 10% of the global workforce - to demonstrate to its consumers that it can self-regulate itself. By creating global standards and a transparent process for Responsible AI, executives in travel and hospitality can limit existential business risks and ensure new technologies make a positive impact on the future of humanity.

CO-AUTHORS

Sahar Cain

Sahar Cain has over 12 years of experience in software development and data science. She has a master's degree in Computer Science, with a special focus on Machine Learning and Artificial Intelligence. Her groundbreaking research in physics-guided AI models for drug discovery has been featured in several prestigious journals and earned funding from the National Institute of Health (NIH). Cain's diverse experience spans various industries, including retail, healthcare, and hospitality, which has shaped her into a uniquely creative and versatile tech leader. As CTO at Mogul Hotels, Cain spearheads the creation and execution of innovative technological strategies, setting new industry standards in hospitality tech.

Gurvinder Batra

Gurvinder Batra has over three decades of experience working with leading enterprises and startups across industries helping them drive innovation, harness emerging technology trends and bring cutting-edge products to market. He's a Co-Founder and CTO at KiwiTech, an innovation ecosystem supporting over 600 portfolio startups. Before KiwiTech, Gurvinder served as the CTO and President at Aptara, contributing to its growth into a leading publishing services company recognized among America's fastest-growing companies for three consecutive years on the Inc 500 list.

RESOURCES AND REFERENCES

Employee Ownership

Ferguson, D., Berger, F., & Francese, P. (1987). *Intrapreneuring in hospitality organizations. International Journal of Hospitality Management 6, no.1, pp. 23-31*

Godoy, K. (2018). *In with the new: Intrapreneurship and innovation in hospitality.* Cornell SC Johnson College of Business.

Mogelonsky, L. (2016). *Intrapreneurs are the lifeblood of a hotel.* HospitalityNet.

Molla, R. (2021). *Service workers are getting paid more than ever: It's not enough.* Vox Magazine.

Diversity, Equity, and Inclusion.

Yonah, W. (2023). *Generative AI holds great potential for those with disabilities - but it needs policy to shape it.* World Economic Forum.

Geller, J. (2011). *Global business driven HR transformation: The journey continues.* Deloitte.

Friedersdorf, C. (2023). *"The paradox of diversity training."* The Atlantic.

Frost, S., & Kalman, D. (2016). *Inclusive talent management: How business can thrive in an age of diversity.* Kogan Page.

Mirza, A. (2022). *The end of labor as we know it: Implications for hotel CEOs.* Hospitalitynet.

Nieves, J., & Quintana, A. (2018). *Human resource practices and innovation in the hotel industry: The mediating role of human capital.* Tourism and Hospitality Research 18, no.1, pp. 72-83.

Anne, P. and Johan, N. (2019). *Sustainable Luxury Tourism, Indigenous Communities and Governance. Sustainable Luxury, Entrepreneurship, and Innovation. Part of the Environmental Footprints and Eco-design of Products and Processes book series (EFEPP)*

Kirsty, G. M. Adrian, M. and Henrietta, M. *Great Barrier Reef Indigenous Tourism Translating Policy Into Practice.* Report of the National Environmental Science Program.

Franchise Business Models and business strategy

Survey on Financing and Growth of Small and Medium Enterprises. Innovation, Science and Economic Development (ISED), Tourism branch.

Lodging, S. (2021). *2021 guide to franchising.* Lodging Magazine.

Russell, K., & Kim, B. (2021). *HVS U.S. hotel franchise fee guide 2020.* HVS.

Fleron, A., Singhal, S. (2022). *The gathering storm: The uncertain future of US healthcare.* McKinsey & Company.

Kreimer, S. (2021). *Health systems reap big rewards by acquiring practices, but physicians aren't sharing in those benefits, study finds.* Fierce Healthcare.

Lagasse, J. (2023). *Hospitals' labor costs increased 258% over the last three years.* HIMSS.

Pace, G., Janiga, N., Lo, D. (2020). *The Value of Branding in Healthcare.* Healthcare Appraisers.

Berger, R. (2023). *Private Equity Makes Inroads Into the Hospital Sector.* Globest.com.

Hardwood F. (2023). *Why Sequoia Capital is sawing off its Chinese branch.* The Economist

Employer Ranking

Arpita. (2021). *Infosys Reskilling Employees On War-Scale Via Talent Marketplace; 34% Hiring Via Reskilling.* Trak.in.

Service Profit Chain

Walters, R. (2018). *Reevaluating the service profit chain model: With special consideration to the HRT segment.* California State Polytechnic University.

Hotel Valuation/Economic Trend

Colliers (2023). *2023 Canadian Hotel Investment Report.* Colliers Hotels.

CBRE (2023). *CBRE Hotels Canada Industy Outlook Q3 2023.*

Deloitte. (2021). *The future of hospitality: Uncovering opportunities to recover and thrive in the new normal.* Deloitte.

Deloitte. (2021). *The future of HR in the face of COVID-19.* Deloitte.

Galun, J. (2019). *How can hospitality join the Agile movement?.* Hospitality Technology.

Lawler, E. & Boudreau, J. (2015). *Global trends in human resource management: A twenty-year analysis.* Stanford Business Books.

Pine, B., & Gilmore, J. (1999). *The experience economy: Work is theater & every business is a stage.* Harvard Business School Press.

PwC. (2023). *RevPAR to finish 2022 at record highs, but economic headwinds strengthen for 2023.* PwC.

Simons, R. (2011). *Human resource management: Issues, challenges, and opportunities.* Apple Academic Press.

Sperance, C. (2020). *Accor just restructured the company in the middle of a pandemic: Why now?* Skift.

CBRE. (2023). *U.S. Cap Rate Survey H2 2022.* CBRE.

STR. (2023). *U.S. hotel revenues, profits and labor costs reached record-highs in 2022.* STR.

Globalization

Burke, R., Koyuncu, M., Jing, W., Fiksenbaum, L. (2009). *Work engagement among hotel managers in Beijing, China: Potential antecedents and consequences.* Tourism Review 64, no.3, pp. 4-18.

Garcia-Herrero, A. (2022). *Slowbalisation in the context of US-China decoupling.* Intereconomics 57, no.6, pp. 352-358.

Gates, S. (1994). *The changing global role of the human resource function.* Conference Board Inc.

Ghoshal, S. (1987). *Global strategy: An organizing framework.* Strategic Management Journal 8, no.2, pp. 425.

Kar, A., & Mahapatra, I. (2018). *HR practices & trends: Understanding global HR practices.* International Journal of Multidisciplinary Education and Research 3, no. 4, pp. 15-21.

Kramer, R. J. (1996). *Organizing for global competitiveness: A research summary.* Conference Board.

Prahalad, C.K., & Lieberthal, K. (2003). *The end of corporate imperialism.* Harvard Business Review 81, no. 8, pp. 109-117

Robinson, J. (2001). *Jack Welch on leadership: Executive lessons from the master.* Prima Lifestyles

Roudometof, V. (2016). *Glocalization: A critical introduction.* Routledge.

Roudometof, V. (2016). *Theorizing glocalization: Three interpretations.* European Journal of Social Theory 19, no.3, pp. 391-408.

Ruzagiriza, A. U. (2017). *Does cross-culture human resource management affect performance of international organizations? Evidence from Rwanda.* International Journal of Innovation and Economics Development 2, no.6, pp. 14-28.

Yin, X., Yang, Y., Kim, H., Zhang, Y. (2022). *Examining the job burnout of Chinese hospitality management students in internships via the transactional model.* Frontiers of Psychology 13.

Disruptive innovation

Christensen, C. (2011). *The innovator's dilemma: The revolutionary book that will change the way you do business.* HarperBusiness.

Craig, W. (2018). *The nature of leadership in a flat organization.* Forbes.

EHL Faculty. *Business model innovation: An exciting sector?.* EHL Hospitality Insights.

Heskett, J. L., Sasser, W. E., & Schlesinger, L. A. (2015). *What Great Service leaders know and do: Creating breakthroughs in service firms.* Berrett-Koehler.

Johansen, B. (2017). *The new leadership literacies: Thriving in a future of extreme disruption and distributed everything.* Berrett-Koehler Publishers.

Jooss, S., Burbach, R., & Ruel, H. (2021). *Talent management innovations in the international hospitality industry.* Emerald Publishing.

Laloux, F. & Parker, N. (2016). *Reinventing organizations: An illustrated invitation to join the conversation on next-stage organizations.* Nelson Parker.

Ridderstróale, J., & Nordstróm, K. (2005). *Karaoke Capitalism: Daring to be different in a copycat world.* Praeger Publishers.

Raj, W. (2021). *Running the Agile and Lean Hotel.* Hotel Intel.co

Stadler, C., Hautz, J., Matzler, K., von den Eichen, S. (2021). *Open strategy: Mastering disruption from outside the C-Suite.* The MIT Press.

Wickhamn, W. (2019). *Innovation, sustainable HRM and customer satisfaction.* International Journal of Hospitality Management 76, pp. 102-110

HR Tech, AI and machine learning

Harold, P. (2023). *Closing the AI confidence gap will help us harness its full potential.* World Economic Forum.

Bissola, R. (2019). *HRM 4.0 for human-centered organizations.* Emerald Publishing

May, J. (2017). *Rewriting the rules for the digital age.* Deloitte University Press.

Eddy, N. (2023). *The future of HR Tech: How AI is transforming human resources.* InformationWeek.

Eubanks, B. (2018). *Artificial intelligence for HR: Use AI to support and develop a successful workforce.* Kogan Page.

Guldenberg, S., Ernst, E., & North, K. (2021). *Managing work in the digital economy: Challenges, strategies, and practices for the next decade.* Springer.

Kover, A. (2020). *A new perspective on hospitality: How Hilton uses VR to teach empathy.* Meta.

Meister, J. (2012). *The future of work: How to use gamification for talent management.* Forbes.

Newman, D. (2018). *2018 Digital transformation trends: Where are we now?.* Forbes.

Frankiewicz, D., & Chamorro-Premuzic, T. (2020). *Digital transformation is about talent, not technology.* Harvard Business Review.

Sen, S. (2020). *Digital HR strategy: Achieving sustainable transformation in the digital age.* Kogan Page.

Shivakumar, K., & Sethii, S. (2019). *Building digital experience platforms.* Springer

Zielinski, D. (2023). *2023 HR technology Trends: Talent marketplaces, expanding AI and optimizing existing systems.* SHRM.

Batra, N., Betts, D., Davis, S. (2019). *Forces of change.* Deloitte.

Talent marketplaces

Bersin, J. (2020). *Talent marketplace platforms explode into view.* Josh Bersin.

Gantcheva, I., Jones, R., Manolatos, D. (2019). *Activating the internal talent marketplace.* Deloitte.

Wilson, M., Shannon, M., Moulton, D. (2020). *Internal mobility and talent marketplace solutions: Market primer.* Deloitte.

EY. (2020). *Will HR transformation be the thread that ties value to experiences?* Ernst & Young.

Field, E., Hancock, B., & Schaningr, B. (2022). *Stave off attrition with an internal talent marketplace.* McKinsey&Company.

Fulton, A. (2021). *Learning a new set of skills through a talent marketplace can revitalize employees.* HR.com.

Gantcheva, I., Jones, R., & Kearns-Manolatos, D. (2020). *Activating the internal talent marketplace: Accelerate workforce resilience, agility and capability, and impact the future of work.* Deloitte.

Hameed, I., Riaz, Z., Arain, G., Farooq, O. (2016). *How does internal and external CSR affect employees' organizational identification? A perspective from the group engagement model.* Frontiers of Psychology 7, no. 788.

TNN. (2021). *Infy starts an internal talent marketplace to meet demand.* The Times of India.

Basch, S. (2022). *INTOO's Career Mobility Capabilities Included in Deloitte's Internal Mobility and Talent Marketplace Solutions Report.* Cision.

Carnetec. (2021). *Is your hotel ready to hire post-pandemic?.* Carnetec Brasil.

Marinakou, E., & Giousmpasoglou, C. (2019). *Talent management and retention strategies in luxury hotels: Evidence from four countries.* International Journal of Contemporary Hospitality Management 31, no.10, pp. 3855-3878.

Maurer, R. (2021). *Internal marketplaces are the future of talent management.* SHRM.

Schwartz, J. (2021). *Talent marketplaces and the challenges of 2022: Time for real innovation in workforce strategies.* Alm Benefits Pro.

Smith, L., Kohan, J., & Pilewska, I. (2022). *What stops employees from applying for internal roles.* Harvard Business Review.

Stroh, L. K. & Caligiuri, P. M. (1998). *Increasing global competitiveness through effective people management.* Journal of World Business 33, no.1, pp. 1-16.

Suhag, N. (2017). "The impact of training on team effectiveness in the hotel industry." SSRN Electronic Journal.

Ulrich, D. (1998). *A new mandate for human resources.* Harvard Business Review 76, no.1, pp. 124-134.

Vaduganathan, N., McDonald, C., Bailey, A., Laverdiere, R. (2022). *Tapping into fluid talent.* BCG.

Vaduganathan, N., McDonald, C., & Novacek, G. (2022). *Internal talent mobility programs can advance gender equity. Do Yours?* BCG.

Vaduganathan, N., Zweig, B., McDonald, C., Simon, L. (2022). *What outperformers do differently to tap internal talent.* MIT Sloan Management Review.

Government policies

Martin, H. (2022). *Chateau Marmont agrees to let workers unionize, cancels plans for members-only hotel.* Los Angeles Times.

McNicholas, C., Shierholz, H., & Poydock, M. (2021). *Union workers had more job security during the pandemic, but unionization remains historically low.* Economic Policy Institute.

Hamilton, H. (2022). *Once Upon a Time, 'Waitress' Was a Union Job. Could History Repeat Itself?.* Slate.

Workplace conditions and safety

Dresser, L., Bernhardt, A., & Parker, E. (2000). *The restructuring of hotel jobs and the role of institutions.* Russell Sage Foundation.

Lee, P., & Krause, N. (2002). *The impact of a worker health study on working conditions.* Journal of Public Health Policy 23, no.2, pp. 268-285.

Streit, D. (2023). *Bronx Frontline Doctors Overwhelmingly Vote to Re-Establish Union.* The Committee of Interns and Residents.

Neber, J. (2023). *City's health care labor moment comes at an inconvenient time for strained hospitals.* Crain's New York Business.

Dowell, E. (2020). *Census Bureau's 2018 County Business Patterns Provides Data on Over 1,200 Industries.* United States Census Bureau.

AI and Robotics

Cathy, L. (2023). *Responsible AI governance can be achieved through multistakeholder collaboration.* World Economic Forum.

Ian, S. (2023). *The AI Governance Summit: Key sessions, talking points and how to livestream the event.* World Economic Forum.

Claudia, U. (2023). *4 ways AI can super-charge sustainable development.* World Economic Forum.

Saemoon, Y., Amara, A. (2023). *Emerging tech, like AI, is poised to make healthcare more accurate, accessible and sustainable.* World Economic Forum.

Michael, O. (2023). *Why we can't leave AI to the machines.* World Economic Forum.

Lily, R. (2023). *Australia launches first-ever AI month to promote responsible AI development.* News Medical.

Eurasia, R. (2023). *Global Leaders Advance Responsible AI Development At Governance Summit.* Eurasia Review.

Shirin, G. (2023). Top VC Firms Sign Voluntary Commitments for Startups to Build AI Responsibly. Bloomberg.

Will, K. (2023), Humanoid Robots Are Coming of Age. WIRED.

November (2022). *Humanoid Robots: Sooner Than You Might Think.* Goldman Sachs.

(2023). *How China is tackling the TikTok Problem.* The Economist.

Aswin, S. (2023). *The Dawn Of Humanoid Robotics: A Glimpse Into the Future.* Forbes.

(2022). *Artificial intelligence is permeating business at last.* Economist.

(2023). *The dawn of the Omnistar.* Economist.

Sungwoo, C., Stella, X. L., Choongbeom C. *Robot-Brand fit the influence of brand personality on consumer reaction to service robot adoption.*

(2023). *The Presidio Recommendations on Responsible Generative AI.* World Economic Forum.

,Artificial Intelligence & Responsible Business Conduct. OECD

The Unlikely World Leader Who Just Dispelled Musk's Utopian AI Dreams. The Atlantic.

Matt, S. *China's AI Regulations and How They Get Made.* Carnegie Endowment For International Peace

Marina, H. *When Musk met Sunak: the prime minister was more starry-eyed than a SpaceX telescope.*

Other Media Articles

Beatriz, P., Luna, S., Juan, M. B. and Ana, M. C. *Sustainable Tourism as a Driving force of the Tourism Industry in a Post-Covid-19 Scenario.* Soc Indic Res. 2021; 158(3): 991–1011.

Rishi, S. (2023). *A Slow Road to Recovery for Canadian Tourism Spending.* TD Economics.

(2021). Statistics Canada, *Accommodations services reach a record high prior to the pandemic, 2019.*

Canada 365: *Welcoming the World. Every Day. The Federal Tourism Growth Strategy. Government of Canada report.* 2017.

Government of Canada. (2019). *Creating Middle Class Jobs: A Federal Tourism Growth Strategy.* Government of Canada report.

Government of Alberta (2019). *Indigenous Tourism Alberta Strategy-Strengthening Alberta's Indigenous Tourism Industry 2019-2024.* Government of Alberta.

Rosa, S. (2023). *Temporary foreign workers need more paths to immigration, experts say.* CBC News.

Dawitt, H. (2023). *Canada's Tourism Businesses at Risk of Shutting Due to High Debt. Skift.*

Hamel, G. (1994). *Competing for the future.* Harvard Business School Press.

Ortiz, R. (2023). *Rising labor costs: Drivers include inflation, high minimum wage, and more hours worked.* Lodging.

Bartlett, C. A. & Ghoshal, S. (1989). *Managing across borders: The transnational solution. Boston, MA.* Harvard Business School Press.

Effler, G. (2022). *Third-party hotel management companies facing higher guest expectations as room rates increase, J.D. Power finds.* J.D. Power.

Bhojwani, R. (2023). *Narrowing of bid-ask spread to result in record hotel sales, plus six other predictions for 2023.* CoStar.

Fuller, J., Raman, M., Sage-Gavin, E., Hines, K. (2021). *Hidden workers: Untapped talent.* Harvard Business School.

Fortune. (2022). *100 Best Companies to Work For.* Fortune.

Lewis, M. (2004). *Moneyball- The Art of Winning an Unfair Game.* W.W. Norton & Company.

Rutgers (2019). *Building the Assets of Low and Moderate Income Workers and their Families.* Rutgers.

Gelsi, S. (2023). *KKR brings employee ownership to the latest mega buyout.* Private Equity News.

Dudley, T., & Rouen, E. (2021). *The big benefits of employee ownership.* Harvard Business Review.

Sutherland, B. May 31, 2022. *KKR wins by treating workers more like owners.* The Washington Post.

Morgan, A. (2022). *The Venetian Resort Hotel Casino to launch an 'equity-like' sharing scheme.* World Casino News.

Coburn, B., & Liberson, D. (2023). *The untapped opportunity of broad-based ownership.* Harvard Advanced Leadership Initiative.

Bhattacharjee, Y., & Ferdous, I. (2018). *How Indian Americans came to run half of All U.S. motels.* National Geographic.

Sapong, E. (2012). *The 'Patel-motel' phenomenon; Immigrant entrepreneurs from India, many with the same last name, now dominate the hospitality industry here and around the nation.* The Buffalo News.

Starr, A. (2016). *Here to stay: How Indian-born Innkeepers revolutionized America's motels.* NPR.

Baskas, H. (2023). *That 'bed tax' on your hotel bill isn't going anywhere, but the things it funds are changing.* NBC News.

O'Neill, S. (2022). *Global hotel sector is turning a new corner: New JLL report.* Skift.

Hamel, G., & Prahalad, C. (1985). *Do you really have a global strategy?* Harvard Business Review.

Freedom House. (2023). *NEW REPORT: Global Freedom Declines for 17th Consecutive Year, but May Be Approaching a Turning Point.* Freedom House.

Khanna, T. (2018). *Billions of Entrepreneurs: How China and India Are Reshaping Their Futures and Yours. Boston, MA.* Harvard Business School Press

Zawya. (2019). *Labor Ministry: 100% Saudization of 20 hospitality jobs as of next year.* Zawya.

Printed in the United States
by Baker & Taylor Publisher Services